"I wholeheartedly agree with Shelly Wildman that there is no better word to summarize what God calls parents to do than discipleship. She unpacks in detail what this discipleship looks like practically, while she reminds us that being intentional simply means being willing tools of the Great Discipler in the lives of the children he has entrusted to our care."

Paul David Tripp
author of *Parenting: 14 Gospel Principles
That Can Radically Change Your Family*

"Shelly Wildman has written a wise book that will have a lasting effect because of her graced understanding and application of principled intentionality in raising a godly family. Readers won't find cookie-cutter bromides here. Rather, they will find insight grounded in God's Word and cheerfully conveyed in personal family narrative by a well-read author. This is a domestic page-turner to savor and reread with immense profit during those fleeting child-raising years."

Kent and Barbara Hughes
authors of *Disciplines of a Godly Family*

"Shelly opens the book with a perfect moment of utterly failed 'family devotions.' Bam! She had me. Why another parenting book? To take parents past the 'how' of performance and into the 'why' of intentions and motivations. Wildman does a bang-up job of showing the way to deeper, love-based discipling of our kids."

Leslie Leyland Fields
author of *Parenting Is Your Highest Calling: And Eight
Other Myths That Trap Us in Worry and Guilt*

"Oh how I wish I'd had Shelly's wonderful book as a young parent! Through practical wisdom, deep experience, and honest stories, she beautifully illustrates intentional parenting in a way that will inspire you no matter where you are in your parenting journey."

Kate Battistelli
author of *Growing Great Kids*, and mother of Grammy
Award–winning artist Francesca Battistelli

"Shelly Wildman doesn't offer burdensome to-dos or simplistic 1-2-3 formulas. Rather, she calls parents to prayerful intentionality. Warmly, wryly opening her life to readers, Wildman gives us a window into godly parenting in the thick of soccer season, basketball tryouts, homework, and Sunday morning worship. Despite her many exemplary qualities, Wildman never claims to be a perfect mom—which must be why I love this book so much."

> Jen Pollock Michel
> award-winning author of *Teach Us to Want* and *Keeping Place*

"If you ever feel lost in the maze of mothering—all the advice, all the choices, all the new ways to raise perfect children—pick up *First Ask Why.* . . . This is an excellent resource to help parents understand their role from a scriptural perspective."

> Melissa Kruger
> editor at The Gospel Coalition

"Each page goes beyond sage advice for raising good sons and daughters and gives action steps toward a biblical imperative. By aligning personal experience with an understanding of God's heart, *First Ask Why* is an exceptional resource for nurturing spiritually strong Christ followers."

> Wynter Pitts
> founder of For Girls Like You, and author of
> *She Is Yours: Trusting God as You Raise the Girl He Gave You*

"One kid at a time, one intentional decision at a time, Shelly's view of parenting is the big sister you can trust."

> Lisa-Jo Baker
> best-selling author of *Never Unfriended*
> and *Surprised by Motherhood*

"Shelly offers a beautiful mixture of challenges and encouragement for every parent seeking God's plan for their family. . . . A top favorite on my list of books to share with others!"

> September McCarthy
> mom of ten, author of *Why Motherhood Matters*, and
> founder of Raising Generations Today

First Ask Why

RAISING KIDS TO LOVE GOD THROUGH INTENTIONAL DISCIPLESHIP

SHELLY WILDMAN

Kregel
Publications

ISBN 978-0-8254-4486-9

Printed in the United States of America
18 19 20 21 22 23 24 25 26 27 / 5 4 3 2 1

For Brian
and for Kate, Caroline, and Julia.
You're all my sunshine.

CONTENTS

ACKNOWLEDGMENTS

THE IDEA FOR THIS BOOK WAS BORN MANY, MANY YEARS AGO WHEN my children were young and life was moving way too fast. Only God knew how I needed to sit with the ideas here, live with them, and practice them before I could actually write them down. This is his book, not mine, and to God alone may any glory for this work be given.

I'm grateful for the people God has placed in my path, all of whom have had some influence over me and the writing of this book.

For my dear friends Rebecca, Amy, Kate, Jenni, Harper, Jeanne, Janet, and all the Mom2Mom women—younger moms whom I adore and for whom much of this has been written. You've been my inspiration and my best cheerleaders.

For my early readers, Cheryce Berg, Amy Danusiar, and Jennifer Merck. This wouldn't be half the book it is without your input, and I am deeply grateful for your honest insights and helpful comments. Jon Nielson, a friend and former pastor, also read an early version with an eye toward the theological. Thank you for taking time from your busy work at Princeton to help me out, Jon.

For others who have sat down with me, discussed ideas, and shared their wisdom, I am grateful. Micah Lindquist, your thoughts on prayer and your encouragement have always been a gift. Cheryce Berg, Becky Sandberg, and Nancy Swider-Peltz all willingly shared their stories and their lives with me—I'm grateful. And to Jen Pollock Michel, Margot Starbuck, and Nancy Taylor, who came along at just the right time to share their insight and encouragement, thank you. To my amazing group of Prayer Warriors—people who prayed me through the writing of this book—I'm blown away and so grateful for the important work you did. Finally, to my Redbud sisters—none of this would have happened without you. Thank you.

My parents, as you will read, have had an incredible influence on me, whether they realize it or not. I'm grateful every day for their faithfulness to our family, despite the difficulties and sorrows, and for showing me what true faith looks like.

Kate, Caroline, and Julia, you have filled my life with more joy, more laughter, and more fun than I could ever have imagined. I am amazed by the women you are becoming and am so grateful to have the opportunity to be your mom. Thank you for faithfully following Jesus and for teaching me how to be a better person.

And Brian. My love, my friend, my partner in crime. Thank you for always encouraging me to pursue my calling, whatever that may be. Thank you for always believing in me, always pushing me, always trusting me. I am the luckiest.

INTRODUCTION

THIS BOOK STARTED WITH A COMPLIMENT: "YOU ARE THE MOST intentional parent I know."

We sat around a bright blue table at a crowded Mexican restaurant one evening, a group of friends who were all PTA moms. Our neighborhood elementary school had brought us together, and we forged friendships over many years based on common interests, namely our children.

My birthday was coming up, so each person at the table took turns paying a compliment to me, as was our tradition. It was nice; I felt affirmed. Who doesn't like compliments, right? Over chips and salsa, my friends built me up, yet in that moment I could never have known that Cheryl's words to me would be life changing: "You are the most intentional parent I know."

Really? Me? The most intentional parent she knows? I glanced over my shoulder to see if someone was standing behind me. Surely she meant that compliment for someone whose children obeyed, had good table manners, and possibly brushed their teeth every now and then. What does that mean . . . *intentional*? And how did I, of all people, display intentionality?

She must not have very many friends, I thought.

I was most certainly *not* a perfect parent. I had lost my temper on more than one occasion. I got frustrated regularly. Some days were hard, really hard, and I spent most of my hours reacting to situations rather than proactively pouring spiritual truths into my kids.

The funny thing is that my dear friend Cheryl knows this about me. She knows my flaws and my weaknesses. She knows that I have never claimed to be a perfect parent. Just like her and all my other friends sitting around the table that night, I was just trying to make it to the "other side" of parenting, hopefully unscathed, and with my children still somewhat intact.

I was far from my ideal of what a perfect parent should be. I still am.

And yet . . . that compliment. It came from somewhere deeper. My friend knew my weaknesses and saw beyond them to what I was trying to instill in my kids. She saw something that I could not see: that my husband and I weren't trying to fulfill someone's cookie-cutter ideal of what constitutes a perfect family. She saw that we were looking to the future, or at least trying to. Cheryl saw that we were attempting to envision the kind of family we wanted to be, the kind of kids we wanted to have, and the kind of influence we could have on the world. And she saw that we were trying to make those visions become reality by God's grace.

Let me tell you something—it is *only* by God's grace that I am writing this book, because my early dreams did not include being a parent.

I was never the little girl who wanted to play house and have lots of babies around her. In fact, my childhood play involved making worksheets, lining up chairs, and standing in front of a classroom full of dolls and stuffed animals.

I always wanted to be a teacher. I never wanted to be a mom.

It's not that I didn't *want* to be a mom; I just never *thought* about it. Even when we married, my husband, Brian, and I said, "Oh sure, we'll get around to having kids one day. We're supposed to do that, right?" But first we had other plans: grad school, jobs, and backpacking through England.

We married young—we were both twenty-two—so for the first six years of our marriage, parenthood rarely crossed our minds. We'd talk sporadically about having kids someday, but for better or worse, being parents was not something we gave much thought to.

Until one day in 1991, after six or so years of marriage, when we suddenly realized it was time. Talk about being reactive! We just had an inkling, a thought that maybe having kids should be next on our to-do list, and we went for it. No planning. No forethought. Not a lot of intention.

Soon we were blessed with our first daughter, Kate; two years later we were blessed with Caroline, and four years after that, Julia.

Brian and I knew two things (and pretty much only two things) about parenting in those early days. First, our role as parents was a sacred responsibility to nurture our children in the "discipline and instruction of the Lord" (Eph. 6:4); our efforts couldn't be left to chance. And second, we were grossly ill-equipped for the job; we could not do this on our own.

We needed help.

So we consulted books and sermons and lectures that seemed to align with our thinking, yet many of these resources simply gave us a list of tasks to do. They seemed (to us) to say, "Here's how to raise perfect, godly children" without giving the rationale as to *why*. And frankly, having perfect children was already out of the question. My daughters, I knew very well, came with unique personalities, inclinations, and (ahem) strong wills. If perfection was the goal, I fell far short in my parenting efforts.

The Importance of "Why?"

As a young parent, I fielded a lot of "why" questions, and I'm sure you have too. My three daughters would never settle for the "Do this" command; rather, they always wanted to know why.

"Why do I need to clean up my room before school in the morning?"

"Why should I look people in the eye when I speak to them?"

"Why do I need to obey?"

"Why?" It's the cry of every child's heart, isn't it? When children ask "Why?" they are really asking, "What are you about, Mom and Dad? What is your purpose? Why should I follow you?" These are big, deep, important questions that should cause us to become more intentional.

Kids aren't the only ones to ask why. Psalmists in the Bible asked why. Job asked why. Even Jesus asked why. The great thing is that God isn't afraid of our why questions. We may not always understand God's ways, nor do we always get an easy answer, but asking the question helps us get closer to a purpose. And as parents, we desperately need a purpose because some days are just plain hard. Am I right?

Clarity about our role as chief disciplers of our children came for my husband and me when we simply stepped back and asked why. Why were we doing what we were doing as parents? Why were we involved in the activities we chose? Why were we emphasizing certain spiritual values with our girls . . . and were there others we should consider?

Why were we doing what we were doing as parents?

You see, when we focused on how to parent, we were more worried about external results than internal change. We just wanted kids who behaved the way we thought others expected our kids to behave, instead of wanting to capture their hearts for Jesus. When we started asking why, our purpose became clear—we are called to be parents who raise children who know and love Jesus, who love others, and who will make a difference in the world for Christ. Asking why has guided our choices and involvements, and it has helped us purposefully disciple our daughters. Asking why has brought focus to our parenting and has changed everything about the way we raise our kids.

A Word About Struggling Families

Over the years, as we have grown in our efforts to intentionally disciple our children, my husband and I have become convinced that leaving a Christ-following legacy is our primary calling as parents. Yet sometimes even our most persistent efforts may not bear the kinds of fruit we'd like to see in our kids. I know of many godly parents whose children have chosen to go in a different direction. I can't answer the question as to why this happens; I honestly don't know. I'm not sure anyone really does.

In John 6, Jesus performs two amazing miracles—he feeds five thousand people with just a few loaves of bread and some fish, and then he walks on water. You'd think that everyone who saw these miracles would have followed him forever, yet John 6:66 tells us that many of his disciples turned away and "no longer walked with him." I am sure that Jesus must have been devastated to watch people he loved turn away from following him. Yet he continued in his calling.

If you're a parent of a struggling child, realize this: God knows. He sees your child, and he loves your child more than even you do. He wants the same outcome as you—a child who knows Jesus intimately, loves him deeply, and has a heart that desires to serve him fully. God hears your prayers for your child, so do not give up praying! Even our consistent prayers can be a matter of intentionality.

Perhaps your family is struggling. Or maybe you're feeling alone and unsupported as you seek to disciple your children. It can feel as though you're just fighting too many battles and that hope is pointless. Hear this: God wants to redeem your family. I believe it with all my heart. God uses Christian families today who hold together under pressure, families who exhibit the power of forgiveness, families who are not perfect (what added pressure that would be!) but redeemed. Our world needs you, imperfections and all, to point others to the one who brings ultimate hope and healing.

About This Book

This book is about my own journey as a parent and how I learned the importance of discipleship in my daughters' lives. I have considered an important aspect of my calling as a parent to redirect my child's focus away from me and out toward the world, and I have tried to reflect that focal progression in each section of the book.

Part 1, "Our Charge," sets the stage by discussing what discipleship is and how setting a vision for our family can help us become more intentional about family life. It's all about our calling as parents to make disciples.

Part 2, "Our Challenge," emphasizes the importance of our children's relationship with their heavenly Father—the inward focus of their hearts—which, I believe, needs to be tended to early. Heart work isn't easy, but it sets the course of their lives.

Part 3, "Our Compassion," encourages an outward focus and examines virtues that will help our children maintain godly relationships with others. As our kids' love for God grows, so should their love for others.

Finally, part 4, "Our Contribution," discusses some ways that strong families can bless the world and, in so doing, bring glory to God. As I often say, we're not here to take up space—our lives should bring value to the world around us.

What I present here are just a few of the areas of spiritual growth that Brian and I thought were important for our family as a whole and for each individual child. We have prayed over these aspects of our family life, thought about them, and talked them through until they have just become a part of the DNA of our family. Most people who know us know that these are our values because they see us trying to live them out every day. But we didn't stop once we had compiled these few ideas; we put them into action, looking for ways to strengthen our family even further. Discipleship is an ongoing effort and will continue as long as we are blessed to be parents.

Here's what I know: your family is different from ours. (I hope it is, because we're kind of loud and obnoxious when we're together, and the thought of every family being like ours is frankly frightening to me.) I understand and celebrate that each family is as unique as the children within it and that each family thrives with its own set of convictions and challenges. Because of this, the way we parent our kids and do family life will vary from one family to the next.

You may find that some areas of discipleship that I've highlighted here are not those you would choose to emphasize in your family. That's OK. Remember that we're all different, and God gave our families different personalities and challenges. Thankfully, the principles in God's Word never change; they are accessible to all of us and still apply today to each of our diverse family situations. My desire is that you will understand and embrace the uniqueness of God's purpose for *your* family.

So as you read this book, think and pray over what you want to teach your child about faith in Christ and what areas of discipleship will be most important for him or her. Think about the vision you have for your kids and for your family. Think carefully about how you might share the love of Christ with those around you who may be hurting. Think about how your family might make a difference in your church, your community, and your world.

And as you begin to define your unique family and disciple your unique children, first ask why.

PART 1

Our Charge

Go therefore and make disciples.
MATTHEW 28:19

DISCIPLESHIP 101

From Failure to Freedom

THE SAME SCENARIO PLAYED OUT TIME AFTER TIME IN OUR HOME when our girls were young. Our family of five sits around the dinner table to enjoy a meal. Sort of. With three little girls, it's hard to get anyone to actually sit their bottoms in a chair for five minutes, let alone through an entire meal. And as far as *enjoying* that meal, well, that's a relative term. Squirmy kids. Picky eaters. Long days. I'll just be honest and say that dinnertime with little kids isn't always the Ozzie-and-Harriet scenario I want it to be.

So there we are, just trying to get through another meal, when my husband looks at me and says, "Should we try it tonight?" I know what he means because we've talked about this so many times I could recite it by memory.

Family devotions. The concept fills us with both anticipation and dread.

Anticipation, because tonight might be the night we have a breakthrough. What if tonight one of the girls "gets it" and begins to appreciate what we are trying to do?

Dread, because we're pretty sure we know how this will go down. We've traveled the family devotions road before, usually with a crash-and-burn ending. Why can't we seem to get this right? Why do these few moments never go as well as we hoped? And our biggest fear: *Are we failing our kids?*

My husband, Brian, and I both think having family devotions is some-thing we're supposed to do after dinner. It has been ingrained in us since before we even had kids. Every good Christian family has devotions. After dinner. Every night.

Right?

Except us. We can't seem to make it work. One girl is too young and keeps getting up from the table, even though we've told her a hundred times to stay in her seat. Another is crying because she hates peas and doesn't want to eat them and we're making her. Another is eager to learn but keeps talking over her sisters.

With each passing non-family-devotional day, our guilt mounts.

Brian grabs the devotional book we've been working through for the past year—I think we're on chapter 2. He starts to read. Julia jumps from the table to let the dog out. Caroline moves the peas around on her plate. Kate is engaged . . . maybe just a little too engaged since she's the only one talking.

Finally, Dad gets frustrated and puts the book away. "We'll try it again another time," he says, his slumped shoulders revealing his defeat.

I'm just over it. Between trying to wrangle the kids to sit in their chairs and act interested in what should be a precious family moment, all I can think about is how late it's going to be before I get the mess from dinner cleaned up. And the homework done. Never mind piano practice.

Brian and I have discussed our mutual concerns about the family devotions scenario. Why are we trying to fit this square peg into a round hole? Will we ruin our kids forever by forcing family devotions? Is this what discipleship looks like? Why should we bother?

 We know that we bear the responsibility of teaching our children about Jesus—we feel it deeply. But what exactly does that look like? What *should* it look like? All we know is that it doesn't look like the scene around our table after dinner.

o O o

Later, I scan my memory of the New Testament. Jesus had disciples. What did he do?

I remember a dinnertime scene in which Jesus taught his disciples, but he didn't open a book or read from a set of ancient scrolls. You know what he did? He stooped down and washed the disciples' feet (John 13:1–9). He instructed them by showing them what a life lived with him looked like. In that instance, it looked like service.

Sure, there were other meals and other moments of discipleship in the New Testament, but for some reason I cannot think of a single scene in which Jesus and his friends stopped to read the Bible, or perhaps a devotional book, and discuss what it meant after they finished eating a meal. Not one.

What I see in the Bible are many scenes of Jesus and his disciples walking down a road or through a field or in a village. Living life. And then something would happen, and Jesus would stop what he was doing to tell the disciples how the situation fit with what Christ had come to do. He would explain the gospel in everyday terms so his disciples would understand it.

> **Jesus understood that the best time to teach was when his disciples were listening.**

Yes, Jesus explained the Scriptures; he did a lot of Scripture teaching. But I don't see his teaching as structured time right after dinner when people are tired, worn-out from their day, thinking about the homework that needs to be done or the instruments that still need practicing. I think Jesus understood that the best time to teach was when his disciples were listening.

A Parent's Number One Role

Thinking of Jesus and his disciples brings me to the focus of this book: discipleship. I believe with all my heart that parents are and should be the primary influence in the lives of their children, especially where matters of faith are involved. I want for my children what Paul wanted for the Colossians when he wrote, "Therefore, as you received Christ

Jesus the Lord, so walk in him, rooted and built up in him and established in the faith, just as you were taught, abounding in thanksgiving" (Col. 2:6–7). Paul feels burdened that the Colossian people, now that they have heard the truth about Jesus, grow in Christ, and throughout the book he offers several suggestions about what that life in Christ should look like in their lives. My job as a parent is to bring the truth of Christ to my children every day, and to intentionally guide them throughout their lives so that they will grow deep roots of faith. That's discipleship.

In this book, we will look closely at several areas of discipleship, particularly discipleship with intentionality. Because without intentionality we may very well feel as though we're treading water, never really getting anywhere, and, on most days, like a failure.

Discipleship, in its simplest terms, means teaching and learning the basic principles of faith. There are those who teach, who disciple (a verb), and there are those who learn, who are disciples (a noun). This discipleship scenario implies a relationship between those who teach and those who learn, and it also implies a subject matter that is deeply important to both.

When we take our babies home from the hospital, in fact the moment we become parents, we become disciplers, whether we realize it or not. Our primary responsibility is to teach our children to follow Jesus throughout their lives. *How* discipleship happens is different for everyone because no two families are alike. *Why* discipleship matters is the issue I want us to think deeply about in this book.

Please hear me: I do believe there is a place for discussion and Bible reading as a family. I do not want to discount that or discourage you from trying to have family devotions. Some of our sweetest family memories are of seasons when we memorized large passages of Scripture together.

On one memorable occasion, we unintentionally left our youngest out of the experience; I guess we thought she was too young to memorize Scripture, let alone Psalm 19. But one day, as we asked each of our two oldest daughters to recite a few verses of the psalm, three-year-old Julia got our attention and said, "Could I try it too?" To our amazement, Julia stood and, with her sweet little-girl lisp, clearly recited, "The heavens declare the glory of God; the skies proclaim the work of his hands. Day after day they pour forth speech; night after night they reveal knowledge" (vv. 1–2 NIV).

Four mouths hung open as our youngest taught *us* something about God's Word—it penetrates even the youngest of hearts. Our baby girl was listening to and absorbing God's Word because of those moments around our kitchen table. So, no, I would never try to discourage you from structured family devotional moments.

But in our discouragement over how things usually went in our family, Brian and I felt that we were failing our daughters or that somehow we were missing something. As we talked and talked and talked about how we could best teach our daughters what our faith in Jesus meant and how it looked in everyday life, we finally decided that discipleship in our family should be so much more than five minutes a day after dinner when everyone was distracted, tired, and crabby.

For me that often meant talking through my daughters' days over cookies and milk at the kitchen island after school. For my husband it often meant teaching our very young girls the great hymns of our faith at bath time or, when they were old enough, enjoying God's creation together on hikes in nearby forest preserves. For all of us it meant talking about important topics of faith while we walked to town for ice cream or, yes, sat around the dinner table.

Enter intentionality.

As our thinking about discipleship began to change, Brian and I realized that we needed to be intentional about how we went about instructing our kids about faith in Christ. We took a step back from the how-do-we-disciple-our-daughters question and started to ask, *Why* should we even try? Because, honestly, there were days we wanted to give up.

Reactive Versus Proactive Parenting

We parents all experience moments that require us to react—our child slams her finger in the car door, gets sick at school, or breaks a bone on the playground. These are unforeseen circumstances that need our immediate attention. But the spiritual development of our kids is not something we should be reactive about. It's not as if we wake up one day in a cold sweat because we suddenly realize that Johnny doesn't know how to pray or Suzie doesn't want to go to church. The spiritual growth of our kids should be something we invest in proactively throughout their lives. Colossians 2:8 is a good reminder: "See to it that no one takes you captive by philosophy and empty deceit, according to human tradition, according to the elemental spirits of the world, and not according to Christ." This verse spurs me on to proactively encourage the spiritual growth of my kids, for good reason. The enemy is eagerly searching for a chink in their armor, hoping to take our children captive for something other than living for Christ.

Intentionality simply means being purposeful or deliberate—something done by design. Words meaning the opposite of *intentional* are *accidental*, *haphazard*, or *random*. When these opposite concepts are considered in the context of our families, I know which I want. When I think of my children learning the most important aspects of my faith, I certainly don't want it to be an accidental process that's left to chance. Proactive parents are those who are intentional about instilling the gospel into the hearts and lives of their children.

God's Purpose for Our Families

What if we intentionally set aside the world's distractions and took time to think about our kids—their personalities, their needs, their unique place in our family? What if we became convinced that our family is important enough to think about strategically? Because it is, you know. God didn't give us families just so we can all live together under one roof and have a good time. We know there's got to be something more because, let's be honest, some days really aren't that much fun. Some days the basement floods, and people panic trying to save old pictures and books. Some days the washing machine breaks, or our teenager scrapes the house with the car, or our fifth grader just can't get the hang of math. Some days moms and dads disagree. Some days are hard.

Some days a bigger picture, a longer view, is just what we need.

God had a plan for families right from the beginning, and his plan was that the world would see his redemptive process lived out in our messy families every day, in all its glory. Restoration, reconciliation, redemption—it's all there within the four walls of our home. When we mess up, when our relationships are broken within the family, we ask for forgiveness and are restored to one another. When we disagree but try hard to see each other's perspectives, we become reconciled to one another. When we show grace to one another, our relationships are redeemed for the sake of Christ. And the world sees.

Our families are a flesh-and-blood picture of the gospel. When our neighbors see us living out our messy day-to-day lives, they get a small glimpse into what Jesus has done for us. God doesn't expect our families to be perfect, but he does want us to know that we are here for something more than mere shared existence. He wants us to shine the light of Jesus into the dark corners of the world, and sometimes he uses our families to hold the lantern. Our effectiveness depends on our intentionality.

How the Bible Helps Me Understand Discipleship

It might seem a little strange, but the book of Deuteronomy is one of my favorite books of the Bible. (Stay with me here!) See, Deuteronomy follows Leviticus and Numbers, two books that lay out the hundreds, if not thousands, of rules for the Israelites' worship—rules that are impossible for humans to follow, rules that, in light of the New Testament, point us to the need for a Savior.

But here in Deuteronomy—and this is why I like it so much—we find out *why* it's important to follow God's rules: "Hear, O Israel: The LORD our God, the LORD is one. You shall love the LORD your God with all your heart and with all your soul and with all your might" (Deut. 6:4–5).

Why were the people of Israel commanded to follow the rules that Moses had shared with them? Because the Lord, the God of Israel, who had led his people out of slavery in Egypt, is a holy God, deserving of their (and our) complete devotion. As a parent, I wonder how on earth I am supposed to teach this to my children. It feels like a pretty big task, an important lesson, and something that might take some time.

Thankfully, Moses continues: "And these words that I command you today shall be on your heart. You shall teach them diligently to your children, and shall talk of them when you sit in your house, and when you walk by the way, and when you lie down, and when you rise" (Deut. 6:6–7).

Suddenly, everything clicks into place for me. Discipleship of my children is not simply a five-minute devotional after dinner (thank goodness); discipleship happens all day long—when we are at home, when we care for our pets, when we get ready for bed, when we eat breakfast. Discipleship is meant to dig its roots deep into the hearts of my children and change them.

Discipleship happens all day long.

Discipleship is intentional.

As the book of Deuteronomy unfolds, Moses reminds the people of Israel of the rules he laid out for them in Leviticus and Numbers, the rules for living a holy life. Once he has finished instructing (or you could say "discipling") the people, Moses again answers the why question, in chapter 30, where we find some of my favorite verses in all Scripture. These are verses that remind me over and over again why I do what I do as a parent. They are verses that help orient my thinking and guide my choices as I teach my children how to live a life of faith: "Today I have given you the choice between life and death, between blessings and curses. Now I call on heaven and earth to witness the choice you make. Oh, that you would choose life, so that you and your descendants might live! You can make this choice by loving the LORD your God, obeying him, and committing yourself firmly to him" (Deut. 30:19–20 NLT).

Here we find a loving God who desires good things for his children. Here we see that, as his children, we have a choice to make—we can choose either life or death, blessings or curses. As a parent, I want so much for my children to choose life, an abundant life, a life of following Jesus wherever he calls them to go. I want their lives to be fully committed to him. And so, as a parent, it is my responsibility to help guide them toward this life intentionally.

This guidance takes on so many forms and will look different in every family. But the best way to begin to figure out how it will look for your family is to first ask why.

Why Intentionality Is Important

There are many reasons to purposefully and proactively nurture the spiritual development of our children, but let me highlight two that have guided my thinking as I've raised my daughters.

First, our culture needs Christian kids who grow into Christian adults who can shine the light of Jesus in a dying world. Just read the headlines—our world is in bad shape. Yet God isn't surprised by what's going on; as God's people, we are called to bring hope. As a parent, I feel the weight of responsibility to raise up a new generation that can speak hope into the lives of peers, coworkers, and neighbors. I cannot quit in this endeavor, so I intentionally pour my efforts into nurturing my daughters' faith for the sake of the gospel.

Second, intentionality is critical because our kids won't just "get it" through osmosis—they have to see us model our faith every day. As I said earlier, I can't just leave discipleship to chance; I've got to show my kids that my faith is real, that God is at work, and that the gospel is true. I do this by choosing, each day, to model a genuine, authentic faith in God. As Paul Tripp says, "I don't mean that parents should 'preach' to their children in the Sunday-morning-sermon style. I mean you should look every day for every opportunity to point your needy kids to the presence, promises, power, and grace of Jesus."[1] Discipling our kids means modeling what true faith looks like.

o O o

I had lunch one day with a mom from my Bible study small group. She has four very young children; her hands are full, and she's tired. As we talked about raising these little gifts, she told me that she didn't read many parenting books and confessed that she's never finished one because she didn't like the idea of someone giving her pat answers for her children. I understand her frustration. My friend said, "I don't need anyone to tell me how to be a good parent. Our family is unique. I want someone to challenge me to think ahead and work within the uniqueness of our family."

Exactly! Within the pages of this book, I want to encourage you to look ahead, even if you can't imagine your child wearing anything but footie pajamas right now. Some of the most effective parents I know are those who picture the results they'd like to see in their kids—the fruit, if you will—and then think about how to accomplish those results in a way that works for them. These wise parents know that it may take years to see fruit, but the effort will be worth it. *How* parents go about nurturing that fruit may look different in every family. God has given each of us different personalities, gifts, and challenges, so why would we assume that parenting by a formula would work the same for everyone?

Why would we assume that parenting by a formula would work the same for everyone?

Here's a small snippet of what intentional discipleship looks like in our family. Over the years, Brian and I have thought a lot about the kinds of people we'd like to see our children become and what we need to do to help them become those people. For instance, we wanted our kids to understand and embrace God's love for all the people of the world, so we thought they would benefit from a global perspective. We also wanted them to know what missionaries do and how they live. So when our girls were very young, Brian and I decided that travel would be an important part of our family life. Our discipleship in this area meant intentionally traveling with our girls, and talking with them about why we travel. (You can read more about this in chapter 11.)

The most important moments of intentional discipleship often happened around our dinner table, where we'd try to not rush so that we could engage in deep discussions. We'd talk about our days—the good and the bad—and sometimes we'd reflect on what was happening in the news or even dream about the future. With a household of girls, it wasn't hard to get conversation going! Once we took the pressure off and stopped labeling these moments as "family devotions," we all felt free to discuss really important topics, sometimes with a book, usually without, but always with an eye toward seeing God's hand at work in all of life.

As you begin to think about areas in which you want to disciple your children, ask yourself questions like these: Whom do you want to see your child become? What kind of person do you want to see in ten, fifteen, even twenty years? What values are important to you, and _why_ are these values important? These are the questions we must ask ourselves as parents so that we can purposefully lead our children to cultivate lives that God can use for his glory.

Consider

1. What are some ways you intentionally disciple your kids? What are some areas in which you could be more purposeful?
2. What is the difference between being proactive and reactive? How have you been reacting to situations with your children? How would being proactive make a difference as you think about discipling your kids?
3. Think for a minute about God's purpose for our families. How has your family shown the love of Jesus to your neighbors recently?

FAMILIES ARE LIKE ROAD TRIPS

Have a Clear Destination

I'LL ADMIT IT—CHRISTMAS IS NOT MY FAVORITE HOLIDAY. IN FACT, December is probably my least favorite month, because during what should be the happiest, holiest time of year, I find myself harried and hurried along with just about everyone else. I rush; I stumble; I force my way through the month of December, gutting it out to make it to the finish line: New Year's Day.

So it was, one particular year, that I found myself not only caught up in all the crazy—shopping, decorating, baking—but also preparing our young family for a cross-country trip to Arizona. Our relatives are far-flung—Minnesota, Texas, and Arizona—and none of these places are near our home in Chicago, so it's usually a big deal when we travel to see our people.

That year it was our turn to visit my parents in Arizona. We had talked about it for weeks, and the girls were getting excited about spending time with cousins, aunts, uncles, and, of course, Grandma and Grandpa. I was excited about simply relaxing in the sun and putting the insanity of December behind me.

On the day of our flight, we loaded our car with suitcases. Then we strapped our sweet, four-year-old Julia into her car seat while our other two daughters buckled themselves in, and we headed for the airport. Everyone was in a great mood, joking and laughing as we anticipated the exciting airplane trip ahead of us.

About halfway to the airport, a tiny voice suddenly piped up from the back seat: "Hey, guys? Where are we going?" Our innocent youngest child had no idea what was going on, and the rest of us just looked at each other and burst out laughing. How had she missed the memo?

"We're going to the airport," I said. "Don't you remember that we're going to Grandma and Grandpa's house? We're going to get on an airplane and fly to Arizona!"

"Oh," she said. "OK." And Julia settled into her seat with a contented smile.

Somehow, in all the rush of packing the car, grabbing our tickets, and heading out the door, we had failed to communicate to our four-year-old the most important piece of information: that today was the day we were leaving. She was happy to come along for the ride because she trusted us, but she was certainly confused.

Where had we gone wrong? We had a plan, but we had failed to communicate that plan to everyone. We had a purpose, to get to Arizona, but that purpose wasn't clear to everyone in our family. We fortunately had a willing child, but often our kids will have a hard time following us if they don't know where we're headed.

I'm sure you know where I'm going with this. We can aim to disciple all we want, but if we fail to communicate our desires to our kids, we'll have a difficult time getting them to the destination with us.

Strong Christian Families Matter

It may seem as obvious to you as it is to me, but I want to be clear— strong families are essential to society, especially today, and researchers would agree: "Healthy individuals within healthy families are essentially at the core of a healthy society. It is the responsibility of society and in everyone's best interest to help create a positive environment for all families."[1] As Christians living out God's purposes for our families, we have a special responsibility to the world around us, and strengthening our families is one of the best ways we can fulfill that duty.

Sociologists use the term *resiliency* to describe families and individuals who, when faced with a crisis, are able not just to handle it but to "struggle well" and continue to love one another through difficult circumstances.[2]

You may have wondered, as I have, why some individuals cope with tragedy or crisis better than others. There are many reasons, but interestingly, researchers have found that the children who are the most resilient to life's challenges are those who have a clear sense of purpose.[3] These children live in families with established priorities and a clear vision, which give these children a sense of security. In this chapter, I want us to think together about what we are communicating to our kids about our family purpose, because I strongly believe that highly functional families—the ones that really contribute to society—are those who communicate "this is who we are" and "this is where we are going" to each of their members.

Mom and Dad, one of our tasks as parents is to give our kids a sense of purpose so that, as a family, we can weather life's storms. Because there will be storms. No family is perfect. No family is exempt from challenges. And no family will escape crisis entirely. It's just the way life is. We need to build resilient families that can walk through storms together and come out on the other side with a deeper sense of who we are and a deeper faith in the God who walks with us.

Ticket, Please

Our family has taken many road trips throughout the years, loading our minivan with suitcases and snacks and kids. One of our favorites was a two-week trip from Chicago to Yellowstone National Park and back via Colorado. We have so many fun (and funny) memories from that trip—the ridiculously cheesy Corn Palace in Mitchell, South Dakota; the claustrophobic adventure of spelunking in Wind Cave National Park; the Alps-like beauty of Bighorn National Park. I'm sure my girls have many tales they could share from that trip alone.

We may have our suitcases packed and our vehicle ready, but before we take off on a road trip, we need to check one important thing—is there gas in the car? Because without fuel, we won't go anywhere. Or, if traveling by air, we need a ticket—we certainly won't get through security without it. Our trip essentials must be in place before we head out on our journey or we'll go nowhere.

Parents, we are talking here about casting a vision for our family and making the plans to move our family toward our goals. But first, we need to make sure we have laid the most basic groundwork. Because without this essential first piece, we will all simply stay home, never moving forward, never growing, and never making a difference for Christ.

That essential first piece—our first priority—must be to point our kids to Christ and nurture that relationship. Once that most essential need is met, we can begin to cast a vision that will help us build the strong, resilient family that the world so desperately needs.

Why Discipleship?

If I were to ask ten parents about their main goal for their children, nine out of ten, maybe even ten out of ten, would answer, "I want my kids to be happy." Happiness, contentment, satisfaction—these are high on our priority list for our children, if we're honest.

Interestingly, most parents would not name material possessions above happiness. Not many would say, "I want my child to be rich" before "I want my child to be content," because they instinctively know what research bears out: money does not buy happiness.[4] Essentially, we know that ultimate happiness comes from within, and that's the kind of happiness most of us want our children to pursue.[5]

> **God wants the same for his children—deep, inner satisfaction rather than temporary, worldly happiness.**

Good news! God wants the same for his children—deep, inner satisfaction rather than temporary, worldly happiness. In John 10:1–10, Jesus explains how to find deep satisfaction in life. In this passage, Jesus compares his people with sheep—it's a metaphor he uses frequently when he talks about God's children. He explains that the sheep are safe within the boundaries of the sheepfold and that the shepherd is the gate, the literal opening in the wall of the pen, by which they can come and go freely. The sheep recognize the shepherd's voice and follow him to safety.

Yet there is conflict. Jesus warns us that an enemy, a thief, is constantly plotting to steal the sheep away from the shepherd. The thief will use any means he can, even sneaking over the wall of the sheepfold to get to the sheep; if the sheep stop listening to the voice of the shepherd, even for a second, the enemy will creep in and easily destroy them.

Finally, Jesus says these important words: "I am the gate. Those who come in through me will be saved. They will come and go freely and will find good pastures. The thief's purpose is to steal and kill and destroy. My purpose is to give them a rich and satisfying life" (John 10:9–10 NLT). Don't you love that? The shepherd's entire purpose is to protect the sheep so that they will have a "rich and satisfying life." The English Standard Version calls it "abundant life," which is ultimately the gift of Christ himself, his presence, both now and forever. This is why we intentionally teach, or *disciple*, our children in our faith. As Paul Tripp says, "You could argue that the chief reason God put parents in children's lives is so that they would know him."[6] Parents, our job is to lead our children to Jesus, the Good Shepherd.

In her book *Scouting the Divine*, Margaret Feinberg shares what she learned about sheep from a real shepherd. Sheep, Feinberg says, are entirely dependent on their shepherd for every mouthful of food they eat. She relates this to our relationship with God—we too depend on him to take care of us, whether we know it or not. Without his loving protection over us, we are completely vulnerable to attack, starvation, and even death. Feinberg writes, "Without someone to protect, guard, and lead us, we are sheep without a shepherd, defenseless creatures who can destroy ourselves or be destroyed with equal ease."[7] Easily destroyed. That's what we would be without the Good Shepherd to guard us.

Notice something else: the *only* way to abundant life is through Jesus, the Good Shepherd. He is a shepherd who loves us deeply and wants the very best for us. The world—the thief or the enemy—does not offer this satisfaction, and, as research proves time and again, money doesn't either, nor do our possessions.[8] Material possessions will never bring us any sense of inner satisfaction—only Jesus can do that. If our longing for our children is to see them lead a "rich and satisfying life," then we must point them to Jesus. All the time. Every day.

Sheep Without a Shepherd

"Our kids need to decide for themselves," some parents say, but the Bible tells us that this type of thinking places us on dangerous ground. What if our children choose to follow the thief? It is our job to protect our kids while they are under our care, to serve as under-shepherds in a way, and to show them the path to true joy. Obviously, later in life our children will have to make that choice for themselves—children can't rely on their parents' faith for their ultimate salvation. While they are young and living under our roof, however, we must make it a priority to show our children that life is most satisfying when lived within the safe boundaries of the Good Shepherd.

Are you making it your number one priority as a parent to point your child toward life in Jesus? If not, stop here and think about that. Remember that what your child needs most as he or she grows toward adulthood is not financial security; it's *spiritual* security. If you need to take some time to reorient your thinking, do that now, before you go any further in this book.

One word of caution: our vision for our kids should not focus on "good" behavior. Good behavior does come from a heart that is focused on Christ, but we cannot make "being good" one of our objectives. Paul said in Philippians 3:10, "I want to know Christ—yes, to know the power of his resurrection" (NIV). Our ultimate aim for our children should be that they know and love Jesus, not that they behave in a certain way. Oh sure, good behavior makes life easier, I won't deny that—I really wish my kids had never stolen anything or told a lie or punched another kid on the playground (yep!); it would have made my life a whole lot easier—but good behavior should not be our motivation. Knowing Jesus intimately, experiencing the abundant life found only in him, should be our focus.

Mom and Dad, are *you* following the Good Shepherd? Do you know his voice? Are you seeking life within the safe boundaries that he provides? Is your life as fulfilling as you'd like it to be? If the answer to any of these questions is no, then take some time to make sure you fully understand that Jesus offers this life to you as well as to your children. There is nothing more important than taking "hold of that which is truly life" (1 Tim. 6:19).

Why Cast a Vision?

With our essentials in place, pointing our kids to Christ and nurturing that relationship, we can begin to think about how we might expand our vision and affect the world around us. But where do you start when thinking through life's travel plan for your family—the plan to accomplish that vision? If you're energized just thinking about this and you're ready to start jotting down ideas, the starting place may seem obvious. If you've never given any thought to a family vision or purpose, choosing a starting place may feel like an impossible task.

The best place to start is by determining your overarching vision. *How* you will lead your kids to the Good Shepherd and shine his light into this dark world is up to you and may look different in every family. But *why* you cast a vision matters. Since acting out faith can sometimes be a slippery concept, I'm going to turn to what some very smart, very godly church leaders wrote over four hundred years ago about God, the world, and how humans interact with it all. It's some of the best wisdom I know, and I think it'll help us answer our question.

The first question of the Westminster Shorter Catechism is, "What is the chief end of man?" In other words, what is our primary purpose or goal here on earth? The answer: "Man's chief end is to glorify God and to enjoy him forever." I love how simple this is—no need to overthink it. First, glorify God. Whatever we do, wherever we go, whatever we say should bring glory to God. Our families should bring glory to God. Our children's lives should bring glory to God. Our work should bring glory to God. Everything we set out to do as a family should ultimately bring glory to God. There are so many creative ways we can do this, using the unique gifts and talents of each individual family member.

The second part of the Westminster answer is equally wonderful: to enjoy God forever. Think about that! God wants us to enjoy him just as much as he delights in us. Are we giving our kids the impression that following Jesus is drudgery? Then we need to realign our thinking and become convinced that following Jesus is the only way to find that "rich and satisfying life" spoken of in John 10. Further, "forever" implies that we can enjoy God eternally. This helps us set our focus on what's really important, on something that will last.

One of the most successful corporations in America, Chick-fil-A, gives us a good example of a clearly articulated corporate purpose that helps focus each employee: "To glorify God by being a faithful steward of all that is entrusted to us and to have a positive influence on all who come into contact with Chick-fil-A."[9] I find it interesting that this purpose statement has nothing to do with selling more chicken but casts a much larger, more significant vision. Everyone in the corporation, from the chairman of the board on down, knows this company purpose, and everyone works together to make sure it is achieved.

Parents, we've got to help our children catch our family purpose, our *why*. After all, we are not here simply to take up space in the world, but we are here to make a difference for eternity. This means that our every interaction—be it with friends, neighbors, coworkers, even strangers— has eternal significance. Our motivations are not self-focused but are intended to glorify God in every way. Intentionally thinking through our family's purpose should give us a view that's bigger than what's right in front of us. Knowing our purpose will reorient our thinking to focus on bringing glory to the Savior who longs to be with us forever. No longer are we simply getting through the day. Having a vision for our family helps us remind our children of what's ultimately most important in this life.

Establishing Your Unique Family Priorities

Planning for a trip is a small thing when compared to planning our family life, yet many people spend more time thinking about their next vacation than their calling as parents. Kids need the security of knowing the vision for their family just as much as they need to know the destination of a long trip. This is why I strongly encourage you to think about your purpose—your *why* question—and begin to establish family priorities that your kids can get behind too.

Now, you may choose to carry your family's purpose in your head or heart, allowing conversations about your vision to happen organically. You may talk about it at your dinner table to communicate what your family stands for, as we often did with our kids. Or, if you like a little more structure, you may choose to write it down and post it where every member of the family can see it.

I love what I read about one family who wrote out their family purpose (or mission statement). In a family meeting, they listed several
defining phrases like "We love to learn" and "We know it's OK to make
mistakes." This list helped them appreciate the unique qualities of their
family. Eventually they were able to take this list and create their family
motto: "May our first word be *adventure* and our last word be *love*."[10]
This simple phrase, written down and posted on their refrigerator, uni-
fies and reminds them of who they are and what they are about. It takes
God's command to love one another and frames it in terms of what
makes this adventurous family unique.

Kids need the security of knowing the vision for their family.

What makes your family unique? No other family is exactly like
yours, with your particular leanings and values. The point is that *you*
get to define your family priorities; nobody else can do that. And you get
to figure out together how your purpose will be accomplished with the
unique personalities, needs, and giftings of each person in the family,
always keeping in mind your number one priority of discipleship. Our
family, for instance, values travel and hospitality, among other things,
but you might prefer pointing others to Jesus through sports. While we
love to watch sports, screaming with the best of them for our teams
(Go Blackhawks!), we just don't have much in the way of athletic talent,
much to my husband's dismay. So playing sports has never been a huge
thing for us.

With our family's purpose clearly defined, we can then decide which
path to take in discipling our kids. There's a host of character traits and
spiritual values that are good and important, but you need to decide
which ones will get your unique family to your destination—to fulfill
your family vision or purpose. The next seven chapters outline the character traits and spiritual values that became important to our family,
but this is certainly not an exhaustive list. The final three chapters of

the book describe activities that we felt would strengthen our family, solidify our daughters' worldviews, and send our children into the world with grace. Basically, what follows are some ideas about how we can point our kids to Jesus and bless the world around us and, most importantly, *why*.

What about you? As you've read through this chapter, perhaps you've started to narrow your vision, realizing that you do have a purpose as a family. Or maybe you've thought about your family culture, priorities, strengths, and challenges. Hopefully, you've begun to think about areas of intentional discipleship that may be important to stress with your kids (but don't worry if you haven't—I've got some suggestions for you!). I'd love for you to stop for a minute and think about how you might apply some intentionality in your lives so that your children will embrace your family's vision. Take some time at the end of this chapter to talk it through with your spouse or a godly mentor, and be sure to include your kids in the discussion. Communication is key!

Remember that God's ultimate purpose for your family is to point the world to Christ. Be a parent who leads your child to safe pasture with the loving Good Shepherd. Tell your kids where you are going in your family and tell them how you plan to get there. Most importantly, remind them every day whom you intend to follow.

Consider

1. List some of the unique characteristics of your children. What are some aspects that they have in common? How are your children different from one another?
2. How can you take the unique combination of personalities, interests, passions, and needs in your family and formulate them into a vision for your family?
3. How does the gospel influence your family's purpose? How might thinking about your family in light of the gospel change what you're focusing on today?

PART 2

Our Challenge

*If you abide in my word,
you are truly my disciples.*
JOHN 8:31

THE PROBLEM WITH TRIANGLES

Intentional Discipline

KATE HAD A PROBLEM WITH TRIANGLES.

For the first three years of school, triangles were her nemesis. They followed her. They plagued her. And they were her downfall every time she brought home a report card.

You see, until fourth grade, students in Kate's school were not assigned a letter grade on their report cards; instead, students received a star for superior performance, a check mark for average performance, and a triangle for performance that "needs improvement."

And on every single report card from first through third grade, Kate consistently received a triangle in one area: self-control.

Kate was a good student—a "star" student in every way but one. And that one area was a big one, in my estimation, so every time a report card came home, I'd sit down with my daughter to talk about how this had happened . . . again. She never had an answer—she just couldn't figure out how, as someone who loved school as much as she did, she continued to struggle in this one area.

I knew where the triangles were coming from: Kate was what I like to call an eager learner. Yes, she loved school, and it all came easily for her. So when the teacher asked a question, Kate was the kid who immediately raised her hand, probably waving it around wildly so the teacher could see her, and most likely muttering, "Ooooh! Ooooh!" under her breath.

She was one of *those* kids.

I'm sure her teachers had asked her to wait before raising her hand. I'm sure they had talked to her about letting the other kids in the class have a chance to answer. I'm also sure she had other issues with self-control, but my eager learner just couldn't seem to help herself.

As a mom, I worried that these triangles reflected a deep character flaw in my daughter, but, if I'm honest, I worried more that they reflected poorly on me. So I harped. I may have even yelled a bit. And report-card time became a time of dread for my girl, even though the stars far outweighed the triangles. What I should have been worried about, rather than her teacher's perception of me, was not so much how Kate's lack of self-control was affecting her performance in school but how it was affecting her relationships with others.

Whatever you call it—self-control, self-discipline, or even restraint—this is an important spiritual discipline that is talked about throughout the Bible. Parents, we must teach our children to have self-discipline because this trait will affect their relationships throughout their lives, including, and most importantly, their relationship with God.

o O o

It's funny, ironic even, that I should write about discipline or even worry about my daughter's lack of self-control because sometimes I feel like the most undisciplined person in the world. It's not that my parents didn't inspire a sense of discipline in me—they did. In fact, they had strict household rules about finishing homework and practicing piano before watching television. The TV was never turned on until 6:30 p.m. after the kitchen was cleaned up and all our other chores were completed.

So when all my friends were talking about the after-school shows they watched (Hello, *Gilligan's Island!*), I just listened quietly because I didn't know anything about the exploits of the Professor and Mary Ann or the Skipper and his "Little Buddy." But my parents had standards about homework and chores, and we just grew to accept them. My parents tried their best to raise disciplined children. And yet . . .

And yet I fail so often.

On many days, my lack of discipline has me getting up late, rushing to get kids to school, foregoing exercise in order to get other things done, leaving my kitchen a mess until dinner, neglecting my time with God. Furthermore, my own lack of discipline makes it easy to rationalize the undisciplined behavior of my kids so that I don't have to do the hard work of instilling discipline in them. Sometimes I just don't want to do it because, well, it takes discipline to discipline.

What Is Discipline?

First, let me say that I am not talking about the old to-spank-or-not-to-spank question. That would be a how question, and that's not what this book is about. There are plenty of how-to-discipline-your-children books out there—some of them very good! So let's put the how question aside and focus on a different kind of discipline known as self-control.

We all know undisciplined adults, don't we? The guy who consistently comes to work late and has a different excuse every day. The college student who is unable to turn in an assignment on time because she didn't get enough sleep the night before. Or anyone who has made the same New Year's goal to lose weight year after year but just can't seem to make it to the gym.

> **God wants us to live in freedom, not frustration.** ✳

We've all been that person from time to time. But what I know from personal experience is that when I lack self-discipline, I get frustrated with myself. And I disappoint the people who mean the most to me, which only adds to my frustration. God wants us to live in freedom, not frustration, so for me, finding my way toward self-discipline is finding my way toward a fuller, richer life. As parents, one of our jobs is to help our kids monitor their own behavior so that, ultimately, they will become well-disciplined adults. Proactively and intentionally encouraging self-discipline in our children not only makes life easier now but also will make life easier for our kids when they are older.

Consider the word *discipline* for a minute. The root of the word means "to train, teach, or instruct." Of course, it can also have a negative connotation: to punish, correct, or control. Let's put that negative idea aside for now and think about discipline as training rather than punishment.

When we dig a little deeper into the meaning of the word *discipline*, we find that it originates from the word *disciple*. Again, the idea of teaching or training is helpful to us as parents. Jesus chose disciples (the Bible tells us he chose the original twelve disciples, and they were his closest friends, but there were many disciples beyond those few), and he spent his three intense years of ministry teaching his disciples, or followers, how to live.

Hopefully, we will have a few more than the three years Jesus had to train our children, but in whatever time we do have, we need to concentrate on the big picture, asking the why question and disciplining (or discipling) our children to become the adults our world needs, adults who know and love Jesus and who desire to spread the gospel wherever they are called.

Does this require some sacrifice on our part? You bet it does! Do kids always get it on the first (or even the tenth) try? No. It requires paying attention, giving our time, doing some hard work of our own, and eventually stepping back and letting them fly or fall, but I believe the hard work of instilling self-discipline in our kids is worth it.

I think my friend Nancy would agree. As a four-time Olympic speed skater, Nancy Swider-Peltz knows a thing or two about self-discipline. One of her children has also become an Olympic speed skater, another is on the US World Cup team training for the 2018 Winter Olympics, and her third is a college football player (and captain of his team). I sat down with Nancy in her home—a warm, inviting space where I noticed a Bible lying open on a table. Friends of her daughter were gathered in the family room, and lots of laughter could be heard in the cozy den where Nancy and I talked. Nancy and her husband have worked hard to raise their children to be not only disciplined athletes but also well-meaning, disciplined adults.

I asked Nancy what it takes to succeed at the Olympic level. She laughed and said, "Well, years ago people thought that simply putting on my jogging warmup was my training. With the media coverage today, people know better." First, Nancy explained to me, she had to set goals, and then she had to get up early, day after day, year after year, and work hard, perfecting her technique until the goal could be achieved.

Was it easy to train for the Olympics four times? "No," Nancy said. "Not for one day." But she knows that to reach any goal, discipline is everything. She frequently tells the Olympic athletes, whom she now coaches, what Goethe once said: "It is not doing the thing we like to do, but liking the thing we have to do."

We may not like discipline, and our kids may not like it either, but eventually we become trained to do those things we must do to achieve success.

o O o

Research bears out what we probably already sense: adults with greater self-control live happier, more successful lives in almost every way.[1] That seems like a strong statement, I know, but stay with me here.

Maybe you've heard about the marshmallow test from the 1960s. Four-year-olds were brought into a room one at a time and seated at a table, upon which sat a bowl of marshmallows. The child was left alone in the room for fifteen minutes and told that if they wanted, they could eat one marshmallow now, but if they waited for the researcher to return without eating any marshmallows, they could then have two. About 30 percent of the children waited, playing mental tricks to get their mind off the marshmallows, while the majority gave into temptation and ate the sumptuous sweet.

In the years since, researchers have followed up with the "marshmallow kids," following them throughout the course of their lives to see what differences occurred between those with self-control and those without. They found that "the four-year-olds who could delay gratification the longest ended up with the best grades and with SAT scores 210 points higher, on average, than everyone else. They were more popular and did fewer drugs."[2]

Research has found that in almost every way—academically, financially, emotionally, physically, and relationally—children who exhibit a

strong sense of self-control become more successful adults.[3] Unfortunately, the children who had not learned the power of delayed gratification and who never learned to be self-disciplined became adults who
"struggled in stressful situations, often had trouble paying attention, and
found it difficult to maintain friendships."[4] Many suffered from a crim-
inal record.[5]

You're probably wondering if the inclinations of a child can be turned
around. Can undisciplined children change? Thankfully, the answer is
yes. Children, even adults, can be taught self-discipline, and willpower
can be increased. In fact, some researchers believe that willpower is a
muscle that can be strengthened with practice.[6] One researcher put it
this way: "As people strengthened their willpower muscles in one part
of their lives—in the gym, or a money management program—that
strength spilled over into what they ate or how hard they worked. Once
willpower became stronger, it touched everything."[7] So parents, don't be
discouraged. Hang in there with teaching your child discipline because,
in the end, research proves that the hard work will pay off.

Why Discipline?

More compelling than research, however, is God's word to us. Galatians
5:22–23 lists the fruit of the spirit: "But the fruit of the Spirit is love,
joy, peace, patience, kindness, goodness, faithfulness, gentleness, self-
control; against such things there is no law." I don't know about you, but
when I read that list, I tend to focus on the earlier gifts—love, joy, peace,
and patience. Those are no-brainers. Of course God wants us to act in
these ways! The virtues at the end of the list—"kindness, goodness, faithfulness, gentleness, self-control"—are sometimes harder to remember,
let alone practice in my daily life. But I can't deny it: if I am walking with
God, I should begin to develop all these virtues, including self-control.

Obviously, self-control matters to God.

But why?

Remember what I said earlier? It takes discipline to discipline. To be
people of self-control, sometimes it takes a little godly discipline in our
lives to hone us into the people we ought to be. And here is where self-
discipline and correctional discipline cross paths. Sometimes parents

must correct children with discipline to bring about the self-discipline that God wants to see in them. In other words, we are, in some small way, exhibiting God's fatherly love when we discipline our children for their good.

Hebrews 12:10–13 says this: "For they [our earthly fathers] disciplined us for a short time as it seemed best to them, but he [God] disciplines us for our good, that we may share his holiness. For the moment all discipline seems painful rather than pleasant, but later it yields the peaceful fruit of righteousness to those who have been trained by it. Therefore lift your drooping hands and strengthen your weak knees, and make straight paths for your feet, so that what is lame may not be put out of joint but rather be healed."

Here I see three reasons for discipline.

First, God disciplines us "for our good, that we may share his holiness." Think about that for a minute! God actually encourages us to be more like him. He sees holiness as something to strive for, something that's good for us and for our kids. Because our heavenly Father loves us and wants the best for us, he sometimes disciplines us, even though it might not be the easiest or the most pleasant thing to do. If God wants holiness for each of us, shouldn't we do our best to help our children strive for holiness too?

Which leads us to a second reason for discipline: discipline leads to peace and righteousness or, as the New Living Translation puts it, "right living" (Heb. 12:11).

Have you ever watched the television show *Hoarders*? These folks, many of whom, sadly, suffer from mental illness, live in squalor, unable to throw anything away until their home is overtaken by their belongings and their trash. The show actually makes me somewhat—no, *very*—uncomfortable. Not just because these people share their space with rats (well, partly that) but also because the mess they're living in makes me feel . . . I don't know . . . *agitated*. Just imagining living in that situation, unable to get out from under the piles and piles of useless junk, makes me sad.

I noticed something about *Hoarders*, though, in the couple of times I watched it. Sometimes, in the process of cleaning out their physical space, the hoarders go through a process of reflection, which leads to understanding—and a lot of tears. At first, the process of cleaning out their home is painful—people cry because their belongings are being tossed out, and they realize the state of their home has not been what it should have been. Then as the show progresses, the hoarders begin to understand that the way they had been living was part of a bigger problem, whether psychological or emotional, and they cry as they begin to realize their inner lives need help too. Finally, after their home is put back together, restored and cleaned, the hoarders begin to have peace and cry from the joy of getting some control over their lives.

Did these former hoarders like the process, the discipline, of going through all their junk, throwing out what wasn't helpful and keeping only what was? No, cleaning out the junk and clearing away the clutter is a painful process. But in the end their hope is restored and joy is evident because they are now able to live in a clean, peaceful, orderly home. The key to outer peace in their lives was hard work, and ultimately the resolving of an inner life problem.

We should desire the same peace and righteousness for our children that God desires for us.

Hebrews 12:10–13 tells us that God is deeply concerned with our inner lives, which are reflected in how we live. God wants us to get rid of the junk in our lives and live in peace, both with ourselves and with others—the kind of peace that leads to righteousness. He is intensely motivated to show us what a righteous life looks like, what a life of peace looks like, so sometimes he backs a big dumpster into our lives and forces us to throw out the stuff piling up in the nooks and crannies. Yes, he uses discipline to get our attention. As parents, we should desire the same peace and righteousness for our children that God desires for us; we should be willing to do the hard work of discipline so that our kids will reap the benefits of a virtuous life.

A third reason for discipline focuses on helping others. Verse 13 of the Hebrews passage says that we are to strengthen ourselves "so that what is lame may not be put out of joint but rather be healed." I like how the New Living Translation puts it: "so that those who are weak and lame will not fall but become strong." The point here is that we must work hard to grow in self-discipline so that we can help others become stronger as well. The good news is that we are not left on our own in this endeavor; God has graciously given us his Holy Spirit who, 2 Timothy 1:7 tells us, is characterized by "power and love and self-control."

On the day our first daughter was born, my husband decided to start training for a marathon. It may not have been his best timing ever—long hours of training meant long hours away from home on Saturdays—but it was a great goal and one for which I am so proud of him. Months of training later, the day of the big race came, and Kate and I headed into Chicago to watch him run. Talk about inspiration! Marathons show the best of humanity, especially toward the end of the race when some people sprint with a rush of adrenaline and others, who have nothing left to give, practically crawl to the finish line.

Those who still have energy left at the end of 26.2 miles (I have no idea how that is possible) often reach out and help those who have none. During my husband's race, I observed some runners put their arms around those who were stumbling and lift them, drag them, or pull them to the finish line. After both participants crossed the line, they fell on the ground in a heap of exhaustion, having reached the goal—the finish—together.

That's how it is in the Christian life. Some of us have energy to keep going, maybe because God has strengthened our faith through discipline. Others are going through trials and difficulties that leave them depleted. We who have been strengthened can come alongside our brothers and sisters who are suffering and help them finish well.

It's a beautiful picture, isn't it? And it would be even more beautiful if this happened in our own family—if we were to help strengthen our children so they became strong adults, able to lend strength to others. This is why we discipline our kids while they are young, even when it's not easy.

What the Bible Says About Self-Discipline

The Bible tells of two parents who did not discipline their children: Eli and David.

Eli the priest (1 Sam. 2:12–4:18) had two sons, Hophni and Phinehas, who were sinful in every way. Even though Eli's sons should have known better, they stole the meat that was being sacrificed before the Lord in the temple—clearly a violation of God's instructions. Hophni and Phinehas were also involved in sexual sin. These two young men lived to please themselves, yet their father did nothing to stop them. One day, God told Eli the terrible news through Samuel that there would be serious consequences for Eli's whole household because he had not disciplined his sons (3:13). That very day, God took the lives of Hophni and Phinehas. And when Eli heard the news, he fell backward off his chair, and he died too (4:17–18)!

Even the great King David had trouble disciplining his kids. When David was an old man, his oldest son, Adonijah, hatched a plan to usurp David's throne, even though everyone knew that David had vowed to give his throne to his next son, Solomon. Adonijah caused all sorts of problems for David, and in 1 Kings 1:6 we learn why: "His father had never rebuked him by asking, 'Why do you behave as you do?'" (NIV). The New Living Translation says that King David "had never disciplined him at any time."

I don't know about you, but I would think that if anyone would have had perfect children, David would be the guy. But even David had problems with discipline, and as a result, David's entire family suffered.

What really strikes me, however, is how seriously God takes our parental actions. In both of these cases the Bible mentions the lack of parental discipline, and in both cases the consequences were dire. Parents, saying no to your child or asking them about their behavior may be the hardest thing for you to do, but the Bible is clear that we must instill a sense of discipline in our children. Because God loves our children, he has given them parents (you) to teach them self-control.

What's Required? Sacrifice.

Sometimes, though, teaching self-control isn't easy, especially if you have a difficult child. It may require some sacrifice on your part, and it may take years of hard work and perseverance—and, ironically, discipline. (Remember, it takes discipline to discipline.) Mom and Dad, it might require you to develop your own self-discipline muscle before you can help your child, but it will be worth it.

Our daughter Caroline completed her first international distance triathlon just before her senior year of college (she is her father's daughter, after all), and let me tell you, this amazing feat cost her. Caroline lived with us while she was training, and I witnessed her sacrifices firsthand. Some mornings she would get up early to train, forgoing sleep. On really hot days when she needed to run, she gave up comfort. And on several occasions Caroline said to me, "I really don't want to swim today," but then she would persevere and head over to the pool.

Caroline was confident in her ability to finish the race because she had done the hard, disciplined work of training. Did she win anything? Break any records? No. But the smile on her face when she finished told us that the months of hard work were worth it. Her dad and I were so proud of her, but, more importantly, Caroline was proud of herself.

Let me encourage you today to sacrifice some of your own comfort in order to encourage self-discipline in your kids, because some days, as we all know, parenting feels like a marathon or, on the really bad days, an Ironman triathlon. Hang in there. Do the hard work and make the sacrifices necessary to teach your child self-control. A strong sense of discipline will help your children grow in godliness and righteousness, which will be expressed as peace in their lives. And the world will benefit from their strength.

Consider

1. Why is discipline important? Is it important to include this in your family's travel plan? Why or why not?

2. Are you a naturally disciplined person? What evidence do you have for your answer? In what areas could you be more disciplined?

3. In what areas do you see a potential lack of self-control in your children? How can you encourage them to practice self-control today?

4

HE IS HERE, AND HE HEARS

Intentional Prayer

I HAVEN'T ALWAYS BEEN A GOOD PRAY-ER.

There. I've said it. Praying hasn't been my strong spiritual suit. It's not always the armor I put on daily, although I wish it were. I know Scripture commands me to do it, and I'm working on it, but it's hard to pray!

My husband tells me that when he was young, his mother would gather her three sons around to pray before school every day. He has fond memories of a glorious send-off, words gently spoken to the heavenly Father before he and his brothers entered the cold, harsh world of school.

I tried that a few times. Mostly, I remembered that we needed to pray when the girls were struggling with coats and backpacks, looking for lost shoes and school papers, and rushing to get out the door. We'd end up huddled next to the front door, and I'd mutter a quick prayer that sounded something like this: "Please be with the girls today, God. Amen." And off they'd run to beat the bell.

Not my finest effort or example.

Like I said, praying is hard. But I know it's important, so I keep trying.

What Is Prayer?

At base level, prayer is simply talking with God; it's a way we can communicate with him and he can communicate with us. The Bible has a lot to say about prayer, and as I read Scripture I notice that every godly character had a rich and vibrant prayer life—they talked with God!

Moses. David. Daniel.

Hannah, Samuel's mother, who poured her heart out to God (1 Sam. 1:9–11).

Mary, who, after finding out that she was carrying the Messiah in her womb, prayed one of the most beautiful prayers in all of Scripture (Luke 1:46–55).

And, of course, Jesus was in constant contact with his heavenly Father.

We sometimes think of prayer as rote and stiff. And sometimes it is. But mostly, prayer is a conversation.

What is the first thing you do every morning? Make your bed? Brush your teeth? Exercise?

I'm ashamed to admit it, but some days the first thing I do is check my phone (not a habit I'd recommend, especially since sometimes I get bad news when I check my email, and no one wants bad news before their feet hit the floor).

Maybe you talk to someone in your home—your spouse or your kids. Around here we have little morning exchanges that go something like this:

Me: Good morning!
Kid: Hi.
Me: How did you sleep?
Kid: OK.
Me: Great! What's on the docket for you today?
Kid: Nothing.

And on it goes.

Even though the communication may not be as great first thing in the morning as it is once we wake up a little bit (we are a household full of talkative girls, after all), we still exchange pleasantries. We check in. Because we're members of the same family living under the same roof, we try to communicate with one another; our familial relationship demands it.

And you never know what will come up in the midst of normal communication. Like the bedtime confession of a child who's terrified of tomorrow's test, or the teen who shares concerns about his future. While the vast majority of our talking with God might sound like checking in, sometimes prayer gets downright messy. In 1 Samuel 1:13–16, Hannah was so broken over the fact that she couldn't get pregnant that her soul-wrenching praying made the temple priest think she was drunk. In one of David's most famous psalms of lament, he said he was crying so much that his bed was flooded with tears (Ps. 6:6). And Moses certainly threw his share of temper tantrums (Exod. 5:22–23). Sometimes talking with God gets messy because life gets messy.

Why Pray?

Prayer is obviously important. But is it important enough to show my kids how to do it or to encourage them to have their own vibrant prayer life? Is it important enough to cultivate my own personal prayer life?

Prayer Strengthens My Relationship with God

When I first decided that I wanted to be a follower of Jesus, whom did I tell? God himself. Our relationship began by our talking together, and it continues in this way. As I pointed out earlier, when we have a relationship with someone, we don't ignore them, we *talk* to them.

When I met my husband, we were both sophomores in college, and in the weeks before we started dating we spent a lot of time talking. On one of those early occasions, we were involved in a massive game of capture the flag on the front campus of our school. Students from several floors of our dorm had come together to play and were running everywhere to find the flags and take down the opposing team. In the midst of the chaos, Brian and I found a good hiding place behind some bushes, and while everyone else was running around, actually playing the game, we sat talking. And talking. And talking.

In fact, we talked so much and for so long, ignoring the game going on around us, that when we finally peeked out from our hiding place, we realized that the game had ended and everyone had gone back inside. We simply stood up, brushed ourselves off, and headed back too, never knowing or caring who won the game. I think of that night as one of the first occasions when we really started getting to know one another. I began to see the heart of the man I would one day fall in love with, and it was exhilarating—I wanted to know more about him! I couldn't wait to talk to him again.

The more I grow in my relationship with God, the more I want to talk to him. And as I pray, I begin to see the heart of God. I glimpse his great love for me as he bends near to hear me. I stand in awe of his generosity toward me as I see him answer my prayers over and over again. I fall more deeply in love with God, and my relationship with him is strengthened, as I spend time praying.

I want my kids to have an intimate and loving relationship with God too. A relationship where they can't wait to talk with him each day. A relationship that is bathed in the understanding of God's deep love for them. A relationship that is growing in maturity over the years. This is what prayer does and will do for our children.

Bill Hybels, the well-known pastor of Willow Creek Church in suburban Chicago, wrote in his book *Too Busy Not to Pray*, "God and I used to be rather casually related to one another. We didn't get together and talk very much. Now, however, we get together a lot, not talking on the run but carrying on substantial, soul-searching conversations every morning for a good chunk of time. I feel as if I've gotten to know God a lot better since I started praying."[1] Strangely enough, I'm encouraged when I think that this man, a pastor, admitted that even for him, prayer was hard. But by purposefully making prayer a priority in his life, he encountered some life-changing results. I want to get to know God better too, and that's also what I want for my kids. One of the best ways to do that is by praying.

Listen, I'm not naive. I know what your mornings are like—you're scurrying around to find lost papers and backpacks, just as I was. Or you're feeding kids, grabbing your cup of coffee, and rushing out the door, probably earlier than you'd like. Mornings are busy, especially when your kids are young and serving as your alarm clock on most days.

I know that the hardest thing to do on busy days is to pray, but it's the most important thing we can do. It requires spending time. It requires slowing down. It requires concentration. Prayer is hard work, but choosing to pray exercises our spiritual muscles.

Prayer Changes Us

As I begin to know more about God through prayer, I begin to change. One of my greatest weaknesses is my self-sufficiency (oh, and while we're at it, why don't we just add my pride to the mix?), because when I feel I've got my life pretty much handled, I tend not to pray. What a scheme of the Devil. What a total falsehood! The truth is, we are nothing and we can do nothing without God. My pride says, "I've got this," but Scripture says otherwise.

Jesus told his followers, "I am the vine; you are the branches. Whoever abides in me and I in him, he it is that bears much fruit, for apart from me you can do nothing" (John 15:5). Did you catch that? Nothing! Without regular times of abiding in Christ, I am completely useless as a Christian. This alone should tell me I'd better get praying.

I want my daughters to have the same dependency on God. One that tells them they can't do everything on their own. One that nurtures growth by clinging to the true vine, Jesus, in prayer. One that recognizes that they can do nothing without him. Prayer helps my children abide in Christ.

Prayer Grows Our Faith

As I get to know God better through prayer, and as I realize that I can't handle life on my own (as much as I'd like to think otherwise), slowly but surely I begin to hand over the control of my circumstances to the one who actually *can* handle my life. When I pray I tell God that I trust him to handle things with my kids more than I trust myself. This reassurance that God is our constant help is probably why the writer of Hebrews said, "Let us then with confidence draw near to the throne of grace, that we may receive mercy and find grace to help in time of need" (4:16). We can be sure that when we pray, God will help us. And every time this happens, our confidence in our Savior grows.

Dietrich Bonhoeffer put it so well: "True prayer does not depend either on the individual or the whole body of the faithful, but solely upon the knowledge that our heavenly Father knows our needs. That makes God the sole object of our prayers, and frees us from a false confidence in our own prayerful efforts."[2] You see, God already knows what we need before we even come to him, so we can fully trust that he's already got things handled. <u>Whatever our need, whatever our concern for our child,</u> <u>God's got it.</u> And while we should bring our requests to him, this knowledge frees us to focus on God's character, his goodness, and his love for us. Our focus, then, becomes not ourselves, but God's perfect grace.

> **I want my children to know without a doubt that "God's got this," whatever *this* may be.**

This is what I want for myself and for my children as they grow in maturity. I want my daughters to learn that God can be trusted to understand their needs. I want them to approach God with confidence that he will handle every trial, every problem, every need they may have. I want my children to know without a doubt that "God's got this," whatever *this* may be.

Prayer Gives God Room to Act

News flash: God actually does hear and answer prayer.

George Müller, a nineteenth-century missionary, preached more than ten thousand sermons in his lifetime. He also ran an orphanage in Bristol, England, housing, at one point, nearly two thousand children. Müller lived every moment of his life in faith and in prayer. In fact, he never asked for a donation from anyone; when the orphanage had a need, Müller would pray and the need would be miraculously supplied.

One morning, as the well-known story goes, the orphanage had run out of food. Not a crumb remained as three hundred children sat at the tables, hungry for breakfast. So Müller, ever the man of prayer, stood in front of the room, praying and trusting God to provide for their needs. While he was praying, a knock came to the front door, and the local baker arrived with enough bread to feed everyone. The baker said that he couldn't sleep, so he got up in the middle of the night and baked for the children. Shortly, another knock on the door, and the local milkman stood ready to supply milk for the orphans.

And on it went. Müller was never surprised by the miracles that happened again and again because he simply believed God would answer his prayers.[3]

You know what? I don't need to hear the stories of a missionary to find out about answers to prayer (although, I do love hearing their stories); I just need to pay attention to my own life. A few years ago, my daughter Kate gave me a prayer journal (oh, the joy of having adult children who now encourage my faith) in which I record requests, Scriptures I've been meditating on, and answers to prayer. Seeing how God is answering even my simplest prayers has strengthened my faith in incredible ways. As I leaf through the notebooks I've kept since that first prayer journal, my heart floods with gratitude and humility as I realize that God is right here, and he is hearing every prayer I bring to him. Not only that, he is answering.

As my children grow in their relationship with God, I want them to know that he answers their prayers. I want their prayer lives to be so rich and vibrant that they will not be afraid to ask for even the most outlandish thing because they will know that he hears them. And I want their faith to grow, no matter how he answers.

Several years ago, Caroline and I got a great lesson in prayer. She was about thirteen years old at the time and was saving her money for summer camp. (Yes, we make our children pay a portion of their camp fees. More on that in chapter 9.) After we agreed on the amount she would contribute, Caroline saved her money all year, but just a few days before she was to leave, she came to me with tears in her eyes.

"I don't think I'm going to be able to go to camp this year, Mom," she said. Her face was grave. I wondered if something was wrong—was she sick? Friend problems? I couldn't imagine what could keep her away from this place she dearly loved.

"Why, honey? What's wrong?" I asked.

"I don't have all the money I need to give to you and Dad, and I don't see any way to get it before it's time to pay you." My poor girl was heartbroken.

"How much do you still need?"

"About forty dollars, I think." Now, the child had already saved three hundred and sixty dollars—a huge accomplishment for a kid her age. I was already very proud of her, and I could have easily let her off the hook for the remaining forty, but something told me to use this as a lesson.

"Let's see. You still get one more allowance before you leave for camp, so that will help, and maybe I can think of a few extra jobs for you to do around the house," I said.

She said, "OK," but her demeanor told me she didn't think camp was going to happen.

"And, Caroline," I said. "Let's both pray about this and see what God does. He knows your need. Ask him to help you."

She agreed, even though still discouraged, and we left the house to run some errands together. I had prayed immediately that God would provide and that this would be a time that would strengthen my daughter's faith, but I honestly had no idea what that provision would look like.

We were gone for a couple of hours, and when we came back, I checked the messages on our answering machine. There was only one—a woman from our church.

"Um, hi. This is Cindy. We go to church together, but we've never met. I was told you have daughters who babysit, and we need a sitter for Saturday. Would one of your daughters be interested in the job?"

I just grinned from ear to ear as I relayed the message to my daughter.

"Caroline, did you pray earlier when we talked about your camp money?" I asked her.

"Yes!" she replied.

We talked and even laughed about how God had so graciously answered our prayers—and so quickly! Two weeks later my sweet girl handed me a tattered plastic bag filled with money.

"Here you go," she said. "It's everything I have." And it was exactly what she needed.

I still think about that experience and wonder if God had used it not only to teach my daughter a lesson but also to teach me something. He is listening to every prayer we pray, he knows our needs, and he has promised to answer our prayers. We just need to pay attention.

So why emphasize prayer in our homes? Why strive to have a better prayer life myself? Because when I pray, I get to know God better. And as I get to know the heart of God better, my own heart changes. I am less the person I used to be—self-reliant, controlling, proud—and more the person Jesus wants me to be—completely dependent on him.

That's what I want for my children too. I want them to know that their lives are not their own, that they were bought with a price, and that they need Jesus for everything. I want them to live lives that are wholly dependent on God, lives of faith, lives of trust, because they have seen for themselves that God is trustworthy.

That's what prayer does for me.

Biblical Models of Prayer

Jesus modeled dependence on our heavenly Father over and over again throughout Scripture. The word about Jesus spread quickly as he traveled from place to place during his earthly ministry. People wanted to see him, to hear his teaching, and to be healed. Often these crowds would press in on him, demanding more and more, until Jesus simply had to get away. The Bible tells us that he often retreated from the crowds for the specific purpose of prayer (Mark 1:35; Luke 5:16; 9:18; 11:1).

Jesus placed a high priority on time alone with the Father.

But there's another person in the Bible who serves as a good example of how to talk to God: Moses. I just love the way Moses interacts with God in the book of Exodus. There's something about Moses that I can relate to.

Here's the situation: Egypt had enslaved the people of Israel for many years, and finally God had had enough. He was going to rescue his people and take them back to the Promised Land, and he was going to use Moses to do it. So God tells Moses that he is going to have to go talk to Pharaoh and tell him to let God's people go (Exod. 3).

You'd think that after an encounter with God, Moses would jump up and say, "OK, Lord. Heading over to Pharaoh's place now." But Moses doesn't do that. Instead, he argues with God! It takes the better part of two chapters in the book of Exodus before Moses finally relents.

In Exodus 3 and 4, we read that Moses challenges God's call no less than five times. Can you imagine! First, he questions God's choice by asking, "Who am I?" (Exod. 3:11). Then he asks God what to say if the Egyptians ask who God is (3:13). He protests that the Egyptians won't believe him when he says he's come from God (4:1). He says that he's not a good speaker, "Oh, my Lord, I am not eloquent . . . I am slow of speech and of tongue" (4:10). And finally, he simply begs, "Oh, my Lord, please send someone else" (4:13). God isn't happy with Moses at this point but still patiently answers him, allowing his brother, Aaron, to be Moses's mouthpiece.

What I find amazing is that Moses isn't afraid to speak his mind to God. Whether that's because Moses has already cultivated an intimacy with God or because he just didn't know any better, I'm not sure, but Moses pours out his objections before the Lord.

The great thing is, God always has an answer for Moses and never wavers from his purpose or his promise. "When I raise my powerful hand and bring out the Israelites, the Egyptians will know that I am the LORD" (Exod. 7:5 NLT). And again: "But for this purpose I have raised you up, to show you my power, so that my name may be proclaimed in all the earth" (9:16). Throughout the book of Exodus we read about God's faithfulness to his people, his deliverance, his mercy, and his great love, despite the Israelites' unfaithfulness to him. And he uses an unlikely and sometimes unwilling servant, Moses, to accomplish his purposes.

Some days I feel just like Moses—an unlikely choice to do the job of discipling my kids. I doubt my abilities. I question my purpose. I wonder whether God made the right decision when he made me their mother. What if I prayed something like this: "God, I have no idea what I'm doing as a parent. These kids you gave me talk back. I lose my temper. I don't understand their moods or their minds. Why did you make me their parent and not someone else?" That's pretty honest, right?

But you know what? God has already answered each of my objections. He already knows that I don't know what I'm doing. He already knows my sinful heart and those of my children. He purposely made me their mom, even though I don't understand right now what his purpose may be.

Make Prayer a Priority

So how do I make prayer a priority? I have to see the value of prayer—be utterly convinced of it—and make it a habit if I hope to encourage a life of dependent prayer in my children.

Tim Keller says, "And so when people ask: How am I going to get to prayer? How am I going to deal with [distractions]? I say, maybe you don't believe you *need* prayer. And that is a theological, spiritual problem, and there is nothing I can do except tell you to get your heart and your mind straight on that."[4] We simply have to get our minds around our desperate need for communion with God through prayer, to make it a priority.

Once we understand our own deep need for time with God each day, we will appreciate our children's need as well. And we will want our children to know that they have an invaluable resource in God—to know that God hears and faithfully answers our prayers.

> **Once we understand our own deep need for time with God each day, we will appreciate our children's need as well.**

As I was writing this chapter, my daughter Caroline said, "Tell them about praying in the car," and I knew just what she was talking about. You probably know that kids are often most vulnerable with parents in the car. Sometimes when one of my girls poured her heart out about a problem or a situation at school, I'd think, *What do I do now?* Honestly, the only response I could think of was to pray, so whether we were driving down the street or sitting in the garage or waiting in the drop-off line at school, I'd often reach over, place my hand on her arm, and simply pray. I didn't realize that my spontaneous prayers in the car were making a lasting impression on my girls, but I'm so glad they did.

What do I pray for my children? It would be very easy for me to simply pray for their physical protection as my daughters go about their day—walking to school or work, flying on airplanes, driving in cars. The physical dangers in our world seem very big these days, and it's not wrong to pray for our child's physical protection. But I think there's more.

Even though I may be tempted to pray for acceptance into a certain school or the provision of a job, what I really need to pray for are their spiritual needs—the fruit of the Spirit in my daughters' lives (Gal. 5:22–23). While it's not wrong to pray for the physical needs of protection and provision—God does care about meeting our every need—we have to be careful not to send the wrong message to our kids, one that says we only come to God when we have a pressing need.

As author Christina Fox said, "I don't want my children to treat God like a vending machine or like a fire insurance policy. I want them to have a passionate love for him that is alive and outgoing, bowing to his supremacy and anchored gladly in his gospel. I want them to love God's Word and hold to it firmly in times of uncertainty. I want them to show Jesus to the world. This is what I want."[5] It's what I want too. God cares deeply about our hearts, so my prayer throughout my daughters' lives has been that their hearts would be soft toward God and that they would grow to love Jesus more each day. My deepest desire is for my daughters' hearts to be molded into the heart of Christ so that they will become women who "shine as lights in the world" (Phil. 2:15).

Mom and Dad, become convinced that you need to pray. Become convinced that your children need to pray. Become convinced that God's heart is for you and that through prayer you get to know his heart even more. Become convinced that his ways are best so that you rely not in yourself or your own parenting prowess but on God as you grow in trust and faith in him.

He is here, and he hears.

Consider

1. Why is prayer important? Is it important to include this in your family's travel plan? Why or why not?
2. How have you seen prayer answered in your life or in the lives of your children? Are you convinced that God hears and answers your prayers? Why or why not?

3. Think over the past week. Were there opportunities in which you could have stopped to pray with your children? Look for similar opportunities in the week ahead and take a moment to pray.
4. Do you find yourself praying more for your child's physical protection than their spiritual protection? If so, how can you begin to focus on their spiritual lives as you pray for them?

5

LOVING OUR TEAM

Intentional Worship

TRUE CONFESSIONS TIME: WE ARE A HOCKEY-LOVING FAMILY. WE love watching the Chicago Blackhawks win the Stanley Cup as they have done multiple times over the past few seasons. We own team "sweaters" (i.e., jerseys) and T-shirts. We even crammed ourselves onto a train with thousands of other crazy fans to attend the first Stanley Cup parade in downtown Chicago in 2010.

We love our team!

But if that's the only thing our kids know about us, our lives will be limited at best and shallow at worst. Because here's the thing: some people get their whole identity from their team. Christians, however, belong to another team as well, and our kids had better know it's important to us if we want them to choose that identity when they are out of our care and on their own. That team is our church.

I don't know about yours, but my church is made up of a whole host of characters. There's the church lady who attends every event and prayer meeting, who even bakes homemade pies for the Thanksgiving social. There's the cheerful man at the bookstall, greeting people with a smile and a recommendation. There are the dozens of Sunday school teachers who lovingly teach the Bible amidst the noise and clang of the children's department each week.

And then there are our STARS (Seeking to Always Reflect the Savior), a group of about 130 intellectually disabled children and adults who are also important members of our church body. Each week our teen and adult STARS join the rest of the congregation for part of our worship service. They sit together in the back few rows of the sanctuary, taking part in the service just like the rest of us. It can get a little noisy at times, but everyone in our church has learned to expect the unexpected because our STARS are part of our body. These precious souls teach the rest of us so much about our capacity to know and love God.

Do I know each member of my church well? No. I attend a large church, and it's impossible to know everyone. But do I love these people with my whole heart? Yes, I do. They are my team. As C. S. Lewis once wrote, "It takes all sorts to make a world; or a church. This may be even truer of a church."[1]

Sitting among this diverse cast of characters each week as we focus on worship is one of the greatest privileges of my life. I want my kids to capture a vision for worship and understand the significance of belonging to a church body, because I know that corporate worship will benefit them for the rest of their lives.

What Is Worship?

Worship is first and foremost a response to what Christ has done for us. It's a response to the gospel! In his well-known book, *Celebration of Discipline,* Richard Foster describes worship as "the human response to the divine initiative"[2] and that is what it should be for us. We recognize God's calling us to salvation, which we do not deserve but for which we are immensely grateful, and we respond in worship.

For our purposes in this chapter, I will also describe worship in terms of a local body of believers, a community, that meets once a week. This regular meeting together is extremely important, as the writer of Hebrews points out: "Let us consider how to stir up one another to love and good works, not neglecting to meet together, as is the habit of some, but encouraging one another, and all the more as you see the Day drawing near" (10:24–25).

A few verses earlier, the writer of Hebrews describes what Jesus has done for us and continues to do today. Through his death on the cross, Christ became the sacrifice for our sins and now acts as a high priest on our behalf. Because of Christ's sacrifice, the author tells us, we can have confidence to come before God, not with a priest as mediator but with Jesus himself to do that job (Heb. 4:14–16). Our response, then, should be to encourage each other "to love and good works, not neglecting to meet together."

Our response to the gospel is not only to worship but to worship corporately!

Now, some of you may be thinking, "Yeah, but I can worship God anytime. Walking in a park, hiking in the mountains, holding my newborn baby—all these activities cause me to worship." While I would agree with you that these experiences are important *moments* of worship, I would also say that the experience of corporate worship (everyone worshipping together in one place) is just as significant, according to Scripture.

Here are David's words in Psalm 145:

> I will extol you, my God and King,
>   and bless your name forever and ever.
> Every day I will bless you
>   and praise your name forever and ever.
> Great is the LORD, and greatly to be praised,
>   and his greatness is unsearchable.
>
> One generation shall commend your works to another,
>   and shall declare your mighty acts.
> . . . .
> All your works shall give thanks to you, O LORD,
>   and all your saints shall bless you!
> They shall speak of the glory of your kingdom
>   and tell of your power,
> to make known to the children of man your mighty deeds,
>   and the glorious splendor of your kingdom.
> Your kingdom is an everlasting kingdom,
>   and your dominion endures throughout all generations.

(vv. 1–4, 10–13)

David's heart overflows in worship and praise for who God is and for what he has done. It's a beautiful picture, but not one that David wants to keep to himself. In these verses we get a very clear portrayal of people agreeing *together* about the goodness of the Lord.

David deeply desires that this knowledge about God be passed on from generation to generation, "to make known to the children of man your mighty deeds, and the glorious splendor of your kingdom." And he claims, "One generation shall commend your works to another." In other words, we need to be intentional about telling our children about God's goodness. And we need to intentionally tell them together, corporately. I understand that taking children to church can be a challenge, and may not be one of those mountaintop worship experiences like David had—anyone who has attempted to help guide a five-year-old through a worship service knows there is nothing mountaintop-esque in that scenario! Still, David sees praising God together as an important aspect of his faith.

> ## We need to be intentional about telling our children about God's goodness.

My pastor describes corporate worship this way: "Going to church gets us out of our self-oriented prison. We are forced to sit next to someone who reeks of garlic. We are forced to put up with music that is not to our taste. We are made to listen to truths that we wish were rather not true. All this is good for us. It is not only good for us; it is essential if we are to find joy."[3] David found this joy in corporate worship, and we can too. But we must be committed to it, both for our own sake and for the sake of our children.

What Worship Is Not

We know what worship is, but I think it's important to note what worship is *not* before we get into why worship is so important for our kids. The one thing I want you to take away, the one thing that I hope will change your perspective on worship forever, is that worship is not for my benefit (or yours, either). Nowhere does Scripture speak of the act of worship being for personal benefit—worship is always directed toward God. ¯ not us.

When I go into worship focused on what I can get out of it, I begin to use words like *inconvenient, long,* or (gasp!) *boring.* True confession: some Sundays I get bored in church (my apologies to my pastor). I get a little antsy sitting in my seat—just like the five-year-old next to me. My mind wanders, and I wonder how long until lunchtime. Haven't we all felt this way?

But that's when we've made our personal benefit the focus of worship.

Another thing worship is not is a place to find intimacy with God. Now, before you start to pick up those rocks, let me explain. While I do believe that we often find intimacy with God during a corporate worship service, I don't think that should be our goal—I just don't see that in Scripture. Our goal in worship should be to "ascribe to the LORD the glory due his name" (Ps. 29:2). In worship we humble ourselves and honor God. David said, "Oh come, let us worship and bow down; let us kneel before the LORD, our Maker!" (Ps. 95:6). It is God's character, not a fickle emotional feeling like intimacy, that should elevate our hearts to worship.

One well-known Christian author wrote a couple of blog posts about why he's given up on church. He describes worship as intimacy with God in places other than a "traditional church service," which, according to this author, "can be somewhat long and difficult to get through." In fact, he finds more intimacy with God through his work: "I connect with God by working. I literally feel an intimacy with God when I build my company."[4]

When we worship, giving God our undivided focus, recognizing his glorious attributes and praising his worth, we may indeed find intimacy with God. But intimacy with God is a by-product of our worship—it's not the *purpose* of worship. I would suggest to this author that our quest is not about a feeling of intimacy; it is simply to draw our hearts and minds to praise the One who created us and who desires a relationship with us. While I would agree that we can and should feel intimacy with God in places other than the local church, I absolutely do not believe that God would call us away from regular worship with a body of believers.

Why Worship?

God's Word provides countless reasons for us to worship, but here are a few practical suggestions. First, a commitment to corporate worship gives us a chance to practice spiritual self-discipline. I am so aware that on some Sundays worship can feel like drudgery; our minds may not be fully engaged or our hearts may not be in it. We may feel burdened by a relationship that's difficult or a financial situation that may not be optimal. We may be harried or distracted by our kids. Someone we love may be sick or hurting or all the above. Sometimes it's hard to worship!

Remember how I encouraged self-discipline in chapter 3? This is exactly when that discipline takes effect—on those Sunday mornings when you just don't want to go to church, when you are fed up with those sinful people who attend your church (you can count yourself among them), when you just don't seem to have anything to give anymore. In moments like those, Richard Foster encourages us, "Go, even if you don't feel like it. Go, even if worship has been discouraging and dry before. Go, praying. Go, expecting. Go, looking for God to do a new and living work among you."[5] I believe God will bless you for it.

Second, one of the most significant reasons to make worship a priority in your family, I believe, is to prepare your children to become adults who worship. I know there are no guarantees that our children will choose to follow Christ, but I firmly believe that if we want our children to worship when they are adults, we must get them into the habit of worshipping when they are children, because worship takes practice.

My pastor for twenty-five years, Kent Hughes, and his wife, Barbara, wrote a book called *Common Sense Parenting* that greatly influenced my husband and me when we were raising our daughters. In it they encourage parents to commit to a local church body and to regular worship: "To imagine for a moment that you can raise a godly child with little or no commitment on your part to the local church contradicts common sense, not to mention Scripture."[6] If we want to train our children in godliness, if we want children who worship when they are adults, we must regularly bring them to church when they are young.

This is why author and professor James K. A. Smith, in his book *You Are What You Love: The Spiritual Power of Habit,* calls us to examine our lives and our habits in a new way because, he explains, "Our hearts . . . are like . . . embodied homing beacons: our loves are pulled magnetically to some north toward which our hearts have been calibrated."[7] In other words, our habits show clearly what we worship, and our lives reflect what's important to us. Smith suggests that we contemplate our involvements—are we being pulled *toward* God by the activities we choose or *away* from him?—arguing that regular corporate worship trains, or habituates, our hearts toward God. "First and foremost," Smith argues, "our households need to be caught up in the wider household of God."[8] Worship must become a habit for us in order for us to pass its importance on to our children.

Worship takes practice.

Finally, corporate worship influences our children simply because of the cast of characters within it. The wide variety of folks in our church not only gives our kids a chance to practice interacting with people different from themselves but also provides them other examples of godly adults. (After all, a teen knows her parents don't know everything!) Think for a minute of the older couple who show up faithfully, year after year. You may not even know their names, but there they are at the end of your row, engaged in worship, Sunday by Sunday.

Do you know that the faithfulness of this couple speaks volumes to your child? When our kids see older folks in our churches who have raised their own children, who have persevered through years of discouragement or even doubt, who have experienced joy and pain within its walls, they see that church is where our needs are met and our questions addressed over the course of a lifetime. The very presence of older generations in our churches tells our children that faith is something worth holding on to, no matter what the years may bring.

Barriers to Worship

I understand that there are seasons in life that may challenge family worship. There may be times when a prolonged illness may cause you to miss long stretches of Sunday morning services. You may be traveling for an extended time. And I completely understand that sometimes, when life becomes overly busy and overwhelming, you need to take a Sunday off. Sometimes we face challenges that cannot be avoided, but usually these don't affect our commitment to our local church or regular worship.

But what about other barriers to regular worship as a family? What about that wiggly five-year-old who simply can't sit still in the pew? Or the grumpy teenager who just doesn't want to be there? I'll admit, our very own children can cause us to want to give up worshipping together, but let me encourage you to persevere. Worship is work, but it is work that will one day become that all-important habit that I talked about. I'll admit that worship, especially with young children, can be messy and difficult and distracting on occasion, but teaching your kids the habit of worship early in life will benefit them in the longer term.

And what about cultural influences that threaten our time in worship as a family? Just drive past any park district soccer field on a Sunday morning and you'll see what I mean. Youth sports are a powerful distraction from regular worship, and as a parent you will need to decide ahead of time, proactively, how you will handle sports schedules in your family. Just remember that whatever you decide will communicate your priorities to your kids, whether you like it or not.

Finally, one of the biggest barriers keeping our children from truly relishing worship is our own attitude toward church. Are we eager to worship as a family, or do we convey to our kids that we'd rather be doing something else? Do we complain about the service as soon as we get back in the car? During the week, do we convey a sense of anticipation toward the coming Sunday by talking about the sermon to come or reading the Scripture passage ahead of time?

Make no mistake, our kids will pick up on our attitude toward church. As John Piper says, "The greatest stumbling block for children in worship is that their parents do not cherish the hour. Children can feel the difference between duty and delight. Therefore, the first and most important job of a parent is to fall in love with the worship of God."[9] It may be difficult, especially if you were not raised in church, but this may be the very time God is calling you to learn to worship.

Before I close this chapter, I'd like to discuss church attendance as it relates to millennials, because many parents share a common concern: Will my child make church a priority when he or she is older?

Are Millennials Really Leaving the Church?

We hear it all the time: "The church in America is in decline." "Millennials aren't going to church anymore." "Young adults are losing their faith."

These frightening words may cause some Christian parents to retreat in defeat. In this chapter, I have encouraged you to stay the course, to remain committed to a body of believers, and to be intentional about helping your children love church and worship—all for the sake of your children.

When we think about the decline in church attendance among millennials, we have to consider various factors. The statistics can be confusing.

Barna Research Group states that nearly 30 percent of millennials claim that church is not important to their lives, and 40 percent say the church is "somewhat important or somewhat not important."[10] According to Barna, 70 percent of today's young adults do not see the value of the church in their lives.

Furthermore, "Barna research shows nearly six in ten (59%) of these young people who grow up in Christian churches end up walking away from either their faith or from the institutional church at some point in their first decade of adult life."[11] As a parent of three twentysomethings, that's startling!

Yet, the Pew Research Center has found that, although religious activities among Americans has declined in recent years, that decline is mainly attributed to a group called "nones"—those who claim no religious affiliation whatsoever. The overall decline in religious commitment is not as big as it might seem, however, because 75 percent of Americans still claim some type of religious belief.[12]

So what's the bottom line? Religious interest in America is certainly declining, although maybe not as much as some would have us believe. Millennials are indeed leaving the church, but they are still interested in religion and a majority still believe in God.[13]

What does all this mean for parents who want their children to share their Christian faith and live an abundant life (John 10:10)? As Jon Nielson points out in his recent book, *Faith That Lasts: Raising Kids That Don't Leave the Church*, "Millennials are engaged in the pursuit of the real, and if they do attend church, it is because they are desperately seeking a God who is transcendent."[14]

Nielson says, "This generation, in a far deeper way than the generation of its parents, craves deep and authentic fellowship with God, and with the people of God."[15] I believe the answer to keeping our children interested in church for the long haul starts with ensuring that they have a true, authentic experience of worshipping God and continues with requiring a firm commitment to a body of believers.

Please hear me: I do not believe that weekly church attendance will save our children. I do not believe that worship is a panacea that will make everything go right when our kids leave for college and start making their own decisions about life. I do not believe there are any guarantees that our kids will choose the path of faith that we have chosen. But I do believe that the earlier our children are trained to worship, the greater the chance that they will continue worshipping when they are adults.

o O o

Several years ago, I was privileged to lead a group of high school students on a mission trip to Italy, where we conducted a sports camp for Italian teens. On our last Sunday, we attended a special worship service that brought several churches together in a movie theater. Some of the kids who had attended the camp shared about their experience while their parents, many of whom had never attended church, listened to the work that God had done during the week. Thankfully there was a tranlator to help those of us who don't speak Italian—the testimonies were moving.

The best part of the experience for me was our time of singing together. The songs were sung in Italian, but many were songs I knew in English, so I just sang along in my own language. Suddenly, I was overcome with the image of heaven described in the book of Revelation: "And they sang a new song, saying, 'Worthy are you to take the scroll and to open its seals, for you were slain, and by your blood you ransomed people for God from every tribe and language and people and nation'" (5:9).

As I stood there, surrounded by Italian believers praising God in their own language, all I could do was simply raise my hands and let the tears flow down my face because the thought of heaven was so real, so precious to me in that moment. One day, believers from every corner of the earth will be united, and our sole purpose will be to praise God forever because of what Jesus has done. What an overwhelming thought of standing with believers from around the globe, united to praise our Savior.

Every week we have the opportunity, the *privilege*, of coming together with others to worship our triune God—Father, Son, and Holy Spirit. When we catch that glimpse of heaven, we see what an honor it is to be a part of the universal church. In some ways, the collection of characters who worship side by side in our local churches each week are a microcosm of that someday church.

Don't you want your children to catch that vision and to be a part of something bigger than themselves? Don't you want your child to be an adult who firmly stands for Jesus in a world that would love nothing more than to draw him or her away from Christ? And don't you want to instill the habit of worship in your children now so that they will benefit from being part of a community of believers throughout their lives?

Parents, if we really want to raise our children to love the church and to worship regularly, we must create a family culture that includes a commitment to the local church and to worship. Scripture demands it, discipline encourages it, and our habits reinforce the practice. In other words, be intentional about worship. Show your children that worship matters to you and to your family. Make worship a priority that will benefit your children as they grow into adulthood.

Consider

1. Why is worship important? Is it important to include this in your family's travel plan? Why or why not?
2. How do you demonstrate to your children that weekly church attendance is a delight rather than a duty? Is there anything you need to change about your attitude toward worship?
3. What would you say is your greatest barrier to getting to church? What can you do to overcome the barrier or at least diminish it?

PART 3

Our Compassion

*By this all people will know that you are my
disciples, if you have love for one another.*
JOHN 13:35

⑥

"MY WORD IS MY BOND"

Intentional Truthfulness

"Mom?"

Inwardly, and maybe even outwardly, I groaned. I had put my nine-year-old daughter to bed an hour earlier and expected her to be asleep. And yet, I heard her faint voice calling out.

"*Mom?*"

A little louder this time.

"Mom? Could you please come in here?"

Oh boy, I thought to myself. *What now?* (Have I mentioned that bedtime is my least favorite time of day? I just want to put my kids to bed and have them stay there!)

Julia was persistent, so I opened her bedroom door; I could hear her sobbing in the dark.

"What's the matter, honey? Are you sick?" I asked.

"No, I'm not sick. I have to tell you something," Julia replied.

"OK. Tell me. What's going on?" I was truly confused. My daughter had seemed completely normal earlier in the day. Our time together after school had gone well. Dinnertime was fine. Everything seemed to be fine, so why was she now crying so hard?

"Today during library time, my teacher got mad at me for talking."

I smiled a little, and stroked her hair away from her face.

"Oh, honey, that's OK. I know how it is when kids get talking.

Sometimes the teacher just has to get you to quiet down. Don't worry about that."

I was still confused, though, because Julia's simple story and her frenetic sobbing didn't seem to match up.

"No, that's not the bad part," Julia continued. "Later on, she came around to see what books we had checked out of the library and I told her the name of two books, but, Mom . . . I *lied*! One of the books was a Captain Underpants book, but I didn't tell her."

My daughter began a fresh round of sobs, while I tried to stifle a giggle. Julia and I had talked about Captain Underpants on several occasions. Her teacher thought the books were too easy for Julia's reading level and encouraged her to try something a little more difficult. I thought the series was simply ridiculous.

But I knew right away this wasn't about Captain Underpants—it was about my daughter's conscience. She knew how I felt about lying. She knew that lying was never tolerated in our home. Secretly, I was more than a little happy to see her conscience come to life in this way.

"So what do you think you should do?" I asked.

Julia took a deep breath. "I need to tell my teacher the truth."

We talked for a few minutes about telling the truth and confessing our sins, and how she might approach her teacher the next day. I hugged her hard, telling her that I loved her and that I was so proud of her. I also said that, if she wanted me to, I would go with her to talk to her teacher at school the next morning.

Let me just say here that it would have been easy for me to overlook this last character-building step. I usually don't like to do hard things— it's just not in my nature. As a parent, I find it much easier to sweep these seemingly harmless situations right under the rug than to bring them out in the open and really deal with them. They could stay with the dust bunnies as far as I was concerned.

I mean, what would her teacher think of *me*? How would my daughter's behavior reflect on me as a parent? What if the teacher didn't understand the situation or respond appropriately?

And seriously? Captain Underpants?

None of that, however, mattered in that moment. All that mattered was that my daughter learn that truthfulness is important, lying has consequences, and integrity matters.

> **Truthfulness is important, lying has consequences, and integrity matters.**

In this chapter, we'll take a look at truthfulness in order to understand the history, the biblical mandate, and the consequences that a lack of integrity brings. Parents, it's more important than ever that we raise children who speak the truth all the time, no matter what.

What Is Truthfulness?

Over two hundred years ago the London Stock Exchange opened its doors to investors, citing a Latin phrase to explain one of its core values: *dictum meum pactum*, which means, "My word is my bond." In other words, my word is enough; I will keep my promises; you can trust me.

Now, we might not think of an investment firm in terms of overflowing integrity, especially after reading about recent scandals in the news, but even today, the London Stock Exchange website explains that integrity is one of their primary ideals.[1] This company understands that without integrity, their business, which thrives on the trust of its clients, could not survive.

In 1801, when the London Stock Exchange opened, handshake agreements were common. Individual integrity could be trusted. Corporate integrity could be counted on.

Even into the mid 1900s, people trusted the word of another, a concept that is beautifully depicted in my husband's favorite movie, *It's a Wonderful Life*. Back in the 1940s, when *It's a Wonderful Life* was filmed, culture was much different from culture today. People trusted one another. Business was still conducted on a word and a handshake.

If you've ever seen *It's a Wonderful Life*, you might remember one pivotal scene in the middle of the movie that depicts a run on the bank. The Great Depression has hit the community of Bedford Falls hard, and people are hurrying to take their money out of the Building and Loan. George Bailey and his new bride, Mary, are on their way out of town, leaving for their honeymoon with a fistful of cash. But the situation at the family business changes their plans.

Good-hearted George ends up loaning all his honeymoon cash to investors. When one woman, Mrs. Thompson, asks to borrow twenty dollars, she tells George she will sign for it, offering an IOU. George just looks at her, in the middle of the turmoil, and says, "You don't have to sign anything. I know you. You can pay it when you can."

Sadly, however, lying has become so pervasive in our culture today that most people do not trust anyone, not even their neighbor. Handshake agreements are a thing of the past. "Trust, yet verify" has become our motto rather than "My word is my bond." Integrity as a virtue has lost its value in a culture that prizes fame and fortune over reputation and respect. As we teach our kids to be more like Jesus, encouraging a change in their hearts and lives, we need to teach them what truth is and why it matters.

God Is Truth

One of the most wonderful things about God's Word is that, even though it may tell us some difficult and challenging truths about human nature, it never changes. From its beginning to its end, we can trust that what God has said about himself and what he values will never be affected by anything culture has to say. God himself is the arbiter of our values.

And what does God value? Truth.

Proverbs 12:22 says, "The LORD detests lying lips, but he delights in those who tell the truth" (NLT). The idea behind the word *detest* is not simply to hate something—it means "to loathe, abhor, or despise it." These words hold much stronger meaning than mere hatred.

And think about the word *delight*. God is greatly pleased with people who tell the truth—so much so that he rejoices in them, enjoys them, cherishes them. This is the kind of person I'd like to be and the kind of people I'd like my children to be, people in whom the Lord delights.

A couple of summers ago, my husband and I took a special anniversary trip to Italy, where, in Florence, we visited Michelangelo's famous

David statue. We had seen pictures of this stunning marble creation many times, but none of them prepared us for the real thing. First, *David* is huge—*ginormous*, as my girls would say when they were younger. The size of the statue alone stopped us in our tracks, but then we saw that even the smallest detail of every muscle, protruding bone, and vein had been painstakingly carved into the marble to form the consummate whole, and we were completely overwhelmed.

Brian, not usually an art lover, sat on a bench for several minutes taking in the beauty of Michelangelo's creation. In fact, he may have shed a tear or two. When I think of delight, I think of this moment in the Accademia gallery in Florence, of being so attracted by the beauty in front of us that we could not look away. That's how I want God to regard me—to delight in me as a person of integrity and truthfulness.

God values truth so much that he sent his Son, Jesus Christ, to earth as the embodiment of truth. John 1:14 says, "The Word became flesh and dwelt among us, and we have seen his glory, glory as of the only Son from the Father, full of grace and truth." A few verses later, John writes that "the law was given through Moses; grace and truth came through Jesus Christ" (v. 17). Want to know what truth looks like? Look at Jesus, who described himself as "the way, and the truth, and the life" (14:6).

Unfortunately, we don't have to search very far in the Bible to see an example of the very opposite of truth—deception. It happens in the third chapter of the very first book, Genesis. You probably know the story: at the very outset, Genesis, chapter 1, the Bible tells us that God created the world and everything in it, including the first people, Adam and Eve. Everything was perfect. Adam and Eve lived in the garden under God's rules. They had everything they needed . . . or so they thought.

Until the Serpent, also known as the Deceiver or Satan, put doubts in their minds. "Did God actually say . . . ?" (Gen. 3:1). The Deceiver begins by questioning the words of God, and things spiral downward from there. Satan goes on to question God's goodness and to twist God's words while Adam and Eve stand by, mesmerized, questioning and doubting the goodness of their heavenly Father.

They eat the fruit of the only tree in the garden that was forbidden them—a clear sin against God's command—and immediately Adam and Eve suffer the first consequence of their sin: shame. "Then the eyes of both were opened, and they knew that they were naked. And they sewed fig leaves together and made themselves loincloths" (Gen. 3:7). Later, when God comes around to talk to them, Adam and Eve suffer a second consequence: separation from God (v. 8). A third consequence follows on its heels: fear (v. 10).

Of course God knows what has happened, but he wants to hear it from Adam and Eve themselves. So he offers them the opportunity to confess, asking, "Have you eaten of the tree of which I commanded you not to eat?" (v. 11), and a fourth immediate consequence occurs: accusation. In his guilt, Adam blames the woman and, believe it or not, God himself (v. 12). Eve blames the Serpent (v. 13). And the consequences pile up until the final blow when Adam and Eve are banished from the garden forever.

Their demise began with deception. Satan lied, twisted God's words, and questioned God's authority. Adam and Eve listened to those lies, conjured up more lies, and finally tried to cover up their actions with even more deceit.

Their falsehood hurt Adam and Eve as individuals—just read the further physical curses that God gave them. Childbirth? Yeah, it's going to hurt. Work? It's now a four-letter word to you. Their marriage relationship was also compromised. What had been a beautiful picture of God's perfect provision in their lives now became a relationship based on hiding, shame, and covering up. The story of Adam and Eve shows that the consequences of deception are far-reaching.

I see three important reasons for intentionally instilling truthfulness in our kids, and they all have to do with relationships.

Why Truthfulness?

First, our kids need to practice truthfulness because, as we have just seen, God delights in it; without truthfulness our relationship with him will suffer. First John 2:4 says, "Whoever says 'I know him' but does not keep his commandments is a liar, and the truth is not in him."

Scripture clearly teaches that habitual liars do not really know God. Just like darkness and light, falsehood and truth can't share the same space. We know God hates lying, so when we practice deception, we simply cannot have a close relationship with God. Our job as parents is to lead our kids to the source of all truth, Jesus, and to encourage a growing relationship with him, so we must teach them the importance of being people of integrity.

Second, without truthfulness others simply won't trust us. Politicians are an easy, obvious target here—hardly anyone trusts a politician anymore—but what about ourselves? How straight are our own everyday dealings with others? Do your coworkers trust your word? Can your spouse count on you to tell the truth? Do those with whom you serve at church or in your community know that you are honest? Once trust is broken it's hard to get back. Nietzsche is often quoted as saying, "I'm not upset that you lied to me, I'm upset that from now on I can't believe you."

Third, on a broader level, society suffers when its citizens are not truthful. Today, perhaps more than ever, we need people of integrity in every area of society: business, medicine, government, the church. Human society only thrives when its people are trustworthy. We all want a doctor who will be honest with us about our diagnosis and treatment, don't we? Or a boss who won't pass the blame for her own mistake? Likewise, parents are responsible for raising children of integrity who will benefit the world, the church, and its people.

Will we be people who speak truth?

The stakes are high. The world is watching to see how Christians will act in our world. Will we fall prey to the cultural pattern of lying, or will we be people who speak truth? Believers in Jesus Christ, of all people, should take the lead in telling the truth so that when we share the gospel with a world in desperate need of him, people will actually believe that what we are saying is true.

The Consequences of Lying

We've looked at three reasons for encouraging truthfulness in our children. Now let's look at the consequences of lying. We see the consequences of lying, deception, and a lack of integrity every day, don't we? Corrupt corporate leaders who lie to make their company seem more profitable. The PTA treasurer who skims money from the treasury and ends up in jail. Even the kid in school who habitually lies to his classmates to gain popularity. But all suffer a lack of trust from their peers as a result.

What can we teach our kids about telling the truth that will make a difference in their lives and the lives of those around them? How can we show the damage that lies can cause? We need to clearly explain to our kids that lying usually starts out small, with little consequence, but the practice often leads to bigger situations with much greater consequences.

I've seen some of these greater consequences firsthand, because I was born and raised and still live in the not-so-great state of Illinois. For some of you, just reading the word *Illinois* probably conjures up a negative response of some kind. It's no secret that my state has a reputation for being a hotbed of corruption, which I find really sad when I think about all the wonderful things that it has to offer. Nevertheless, in my lifetime four of our governors have gone to prison. Four! And probably many more politicians in other branches of government. It's a not-so-funny joke here that entire wings of prisons have been built to hold Illinois politicians.

The consequences of deceit have been dire for our state. I don't need to go into the financial problems we face, the social issues that have plagued our cities, or the courtrooms that overflow every single day. The main consequence here, though, is the lack of trust that the people have for those who supposedly serve us. Sadly, their bad reputation has been earned.

What About Those "Little White Lies"?

Mistrust of politicians is a huge issue, but integrity (or lack of it) starts on a level far below that of the government. Usually a lack of integrity begins with an individual who has become convinced that their words don't matter and their "little white lies" won't hurt anyone.

Scripture is clear that lying is harmful, no matter how big or how small the lie (Prov. 25:18). As parents, then, we need to think through how we're going to handle lying when it comes up—because it will come up. No child is truthful all the time. As parents, we need to be ready to stop every lie every time one is formed on our children's tongues.

Author and psychologist Maria Konnikova, who has done extensive research on con artists and habitual liars, agrees. In a *New York Times* interview she stated, "Nothing reinforces cheating so much as getting away with it. . . . Recognizing and talking about dishonesty is better for the kids, and will make them more truthful going forward."[2] Cheaters, liars, and con artists start their behavior when they are young; they keep going because they get away with it. As parents, we must carefully and intentionally cultivate truthfulness in our children because, as I've already said, a lack of integrity in this area will harm not only ourselves but also all those around us and, most importantly, our witness for Jesus in the world.

At this point you may be wondering about those little white lies. You know, those lies we tell each other to make one another feel better: "No, that dress doesn't make you look fat," or "This dinner is delicious," when really it's a charred mess on a plate. We've all told similar lies, maybe even today! While technically these are social kindnesses, and we may tell little white lies to come across as polite, we have to ask, does telling white lies matter enough to the development of character that we should keep our children from telling them? Well, research says it might. Kids who tell white lies at a young age become better and better at lying as they get older. If the behavior is not stopped, many children can become convinced that their lies are actually truth.[3]

Maybe you've been duped into thinking those little white lies our kids tell are no big deal and can easily be overlooked. Maybe you habitually lie yourself. Here's where we all, myself included, need a heart check.

A heart check asks: Am I being a person who speaks the truth at all times? Am I following God's command in my own life to be a person of truth, not lies (Col. 3:9)? Do my words reflect a heart that has been changed by the gospel of Jesus Christ? Am I a person of integrity whom others trust? Because this is what telling the truth comes down to— trust. A heart check asks whether I am being a person whose words my spouse and children can trust. A heart check insists that my words and my actions align.

We need to examine our words and our hearts because our kids are watching. They know what we're up to. They know when we tell our- selves we need a "mental health break" and call in sick. They hear us making false excuses for why we can't fulfill a commitment or show up on time. They see us break promises. And when they catch us acting in deceitful ways, they learn that the truth isn't essential all the time.

Furthermore, are we insisting our children tell the truth at all times, no matter what? Are we calling out lies when we see them? Are we requiring our kids to be truthful in their dealings with their friends, teachers, and teammates? Are we insisting on the truth, even when it's hard?

We're instilling, brick by brick, a pattern of integrity that will build trust in others.

Our personal integrity matters, and our kids need to know that— because just as our kids are watching us, others, like their friends, teach- ers, and teammates, are watching our kids. Are we asking ourselves and our children, "Who are you when no one else is looking?" That is integ- rity. When we insist on truthfulness in our children, we're instilling, brick by brick, a pattern of integrity that will build trust in others.

What Can Parents Do?

First, insist on the truth. Every time. When the issue of lying creeps up in younger children, don't be surprised—it's going to happen. Every child tests the waters. But don't let it go. Call out the lie every time.

Second, make your child promise to tell the truth. Research has shown that kids who promise to speak truth become more truthful adults.[4] Think of that! Just *agreeing* to be truthful makes kids more truthful. Maybe one of your family values could be that you will be people of the truth in all things, all the time.

Third, show your kids that the truth matters to God, that their *words* matter to God. This may be an opportunity to talk to your kids about God being with them all the time (Deut. 31:6), God hearing every word they speak (Ps. 94:9), and God valuing the truth (Ps. 51:6). As the well-known theologian John Piper has said, "Telling the truth is evidence that we know God and have faith in Him."[5]

Has lying become a habit with your kids? Recognize the pattern and stop it in its tracks. Begin today to instill truthfulness in your children so that they will become trustworthy people who can change the world.

Finally, remember that there is grace. Our kids will mess up. *We* will mess up! But God has sent his Son to cover our messes.

Remember the first example of deception in the Bible? In Genesis 3, we read a discouraging account of our first parents. Yet when all seemed lost in the story, just as God was imposing his punishment on Adam and Eve, there is a verse of hope: "And the LORD God made for Adam and for his wife garments of skins and clothed them" (Gen. 3:21).

This verse, tucked into one of the most devastating chapters of the Bible, is to me a verse of profound and, yes, amazing grace. Think about it. God knew about Satan's lies and Adam's and Eve's disobedience long before he confronted them with it. Yes, there were consequences for their sin. But God didn't want Adam and Eve to suffer the shame of their sin, so he did something about it—he gave them clothing. While this wasn't a convenient covering, it was certainly profound because God sacrificed an animal (or maybe more than one) to graciously clothe Adam and Eve with its innocent hide.

Later in the Gospels we learn of another sacrifice for sin: that of God's only Son, Jesus Christ. The Bible tells us that "while we were still sinners, Christ died for us" (Rom. 5:8). What grace we have been given! Even though I can be just as deceptive as the Serpent, even though I may have lying lips from time to time, I can trust that Jesus has forgiven me.

o O o

Remember the Captain Underpants incident? Julia learned a huge lesson in grace when she confessed her lie to her teacher that day.

I have to be honest and tell you that I really wasn't looking forward to talking to Julia's teacher. By the time we had eaten breakfast the next morning, I was pretty sure that this was a stupid exercise. I was convinced that it probably wouldn't matter if Julia followed up with her teacher. And I was certain that her teacher would think we were foolish for confessing such a small thing.

But I put on my big-girl underpanties (get it?) and did the hard thing: I accompanied my daughter to school to talk with her teacher. We prayed before we left, and we walked hand in hand into Julia's classroom where her teacher was preparing for the day. She looked up and greeted us, and she could tell immediately that Julia had something on her mind. As we sat at three kid-sized desks, Julia confessed the previous day's lie to her teacher.

Without hesitation, her teacher smiled and said, "I'm so glad you came to me, Julia. A lot of kids wouldn't have done that, but it means a lot that you told the truth. Now, let's see if we can find a more appropriate book for you to read." In that moment, my daughter experienced the relief of grace and forgiveness. She smiled and sat up a little straighter, as if an immense weight had been lifted from her shoulders.

I thanked her teacher, hugged my now joyful daughter, and walked home with a new lightness in my own step. God had answered our prayer and had gone above and beyond to teach my daughter an important lesson about honesty: there is grace to be found when we tell the truth.

Do you need that grace and freedom? Do you need that goodness? Do you need to confess a lie or maybe be more intentional about telling the truth or insisting on it in your kids? Whatever you need to do to become a person of integrity today or to help your children become people of integrity, do it. Because the world needs you to be that person. The world needs children who will make a difference by their commitment to the truth. The world needs people it can trust.

Consider

1. Why is truthfulness important? Is it important to include this in your family's travel plan? Read the following Bible verses: Proverbs 6:16–19; 12:22; 14:25; John 8:32; Colossians 3:9; and 1 John 2:4. Why do you think God objects so strongly to lying?
2. Have you been insisting on your child's truthfulness at all times? What can you do this week to help your child in this area?
3. Perform a heart check on yourself this week. Ask (and honestly answer) whether you have been the kind of person you want your child to be. Is your word your bond?

7

HAVING EYES TO SEE

Intentional Kindness

A FACEBOOK POST DEPICTING A YOUNG REDHEADED BOY EATING lunch with a very large Florida State football player recently captured my attention. The story told about the FSU team that had visited the boy's school. As the players ate lunch in the school cafeteria, Travis Rudolph, one of the stars of the team, noticed Bo Paske sitting alone.

Sitting alone was not an uncommon occurrence for Bo, who has autism. The kids in his school didn't often ask him to join them at their lunch tables; many probably didn't even notice Bo sitting alone, day after day, while he ate.

But Travis Rudolph noticed. On the day of the team's visit, he walked over to Bo and asked to join him. Bo, a huge FSU fan, was thrilled. The two enjoyed their time together, talking football and changing Bo's life. Because of Rudolph's one simple act, other students no longer thought of Bo as the "autistic kid." He was Bo Paske, and he belonged. And at least for a day or two, our nation focused on kindness.[1]

What does it take for a football player—or anyone, for that matter—to notice an outsider? It takes a lifetime of practice. A lifetime of seeing other people, of looking outside of himself and putting himself in the shoes of another person.

Earlier I read a story about five fifth-grade boys who befriended James, a bullied classmate with learning disabilities. This group of boys—young men, really—pledged to "have James's back" on the playground and in school. They committed to playing with him at recess and eating lunch with him every day. According to James's mother, their kindness has changed his life. Previously cast aside, James quietly kept to himself, but with the influence of their friendship, James is now thriving. He plays sports, he's outgoing, and he cannot stop smiling.[2]

Why do stories like these stir something deep inside us? Why do they touch us in ways that other stories do not? I wonder if it's because kindnesses like these are so rare in our world today. We need to hear these stories. We need to be a *part* of these stories. And our kids need to learn that kindness matters.

What Is Kindness?

Let's clarify something: being *kind* and being *nice* are not the same thing. When someone acts out of, say, politeness, they come across as nice, but being nice is simply a social grace. We act *nicely* because we want to be perceived positively, but we act *kindly* because of a deeper motivation of the heart. Everyone can be nice, but not everyone is kind.

If kindness isn't merely being nice, then what is it? *Kindness* is hard to define today because it is so rare, yet, when we come across someone who is truly kind, we take notice.

In 2015, the college where I used to teach lost a beloved professor whom I consider one of the kindest men I've ever known. Brett Foster was one of those rare people who, no matter whether he was rushing to a meeting or to class, would always take time to stop, look me in the eye, and ask how things were going. We taught in the same department, and though we didn't know each other well, Brett always remembered our previous conversations and brought up small details he had noted. And he always asked about my daughter Kate, whom he had had in class.

Brett died after an eighteen-month battle with cancer. His life was much too short—only forty-two years—yet he left a legacy that was beautifully acknowledged at his memorial service on campus. Long-time friends and colleagues talked about his sense of humor, his love for his family, and, yes, his kindness.

What set Brett apart from so many others? It was the way he noticed, really noticed others. He intentionally looked people in the eye. He stopped to listen, no matter how busy he was. As a colleague from another institution put it, "To be in his company was to be wholly accompanied by him. His eyes would be all attention. His thoughts and words almost visibly dedicated to your own."[3] This was the man I knew too.

Brett made a difference just by being kind, and his kindness made everyone around him want to be better people.

That, I believe, is what separates being nice from being kind. Nice people do nice things, with varying motivations. Kind people notice. Kind people look you in the eye and treat you with respect and honor. Their motivation is simply *you*.

> ## Kind people look you in the eye and treat you with respect and honor.

Scripture helps us understand kindness further. In 1 Corinthians 13, commonly known as the love chapter, we read these familiar words: "Love is patient, love is kind" (v. 4 NIV). Stop right there. Notice that Scripture doesn't say, "Love is nice." How trite would that be! Rather, Paul emphasizes that love is kind.

What does the distinction between *nice* and *kind* mean for us and for our children? If, as Scripture tells us, love is kind and love comes from God (1 John 4:7), then our kindness is evidence of God's love within us, and if Christ's love resides within us, we will treat others with kindness. Period. Scripture tells us that the world will know we are Jesus's followers by our love (John 13:35), by how we treat others. So our kindness, because it and love are so closely related, is a way to point the world to him.

Just writing this is humbling to me. I'm torn between my inclination toward selfishness and my love for God. I get caught up in my own life, my own agenda, my own stuff, and I forget to stop and notice others. But I do love God and want to point people to Jesus, so I will work on developing kindness in my own life and in the lives of my children.

Why Kindness?

So let's get to the heart of the matter: why should we teach our kids to be kind, especially in our cruel and unkind world?

Maybe our first reason is right there in the question: our cruel and unkind world. We all know that the megaphone of negativity is louder than ever and the soft voice of kindness is rarely heard today. When we hear stories of random acts of kindness, like the "pay-it-backward" folks in the Starbucks drive-thru, we all stop and pay attention. It's just so rare today.

I learned a great lesson on kindness from my dad one summer when our family traveled to New York City. It was the first time I had ever ventured far from our farm in Illinois, so I was excited when we dropped our bags at our hotel and headed out to see the great sights of the city. We walked only a few blocks, however, before we encountered a strange and sad sight: a woman had passed out on the sidewalk, completely blocking the path.

Our little family stood there for a minute, trying to figure out what to do, while others simply stepped right over the woman and walked on. My dad would have none of that, so he went to a building nearby to talk to the doorman, but the doorman would not get involved. "It's not my building," he said with a shrug of his shoulders, peering down the street at the woman.

"Let's just go," we urged Dad. It seemed like everyone else had the right idea—keep your head down, don't look, don't notice, and you won't be inconvenienced.

I still remember my dad's words: "No. I am not leaving her here like this."

Eventually an ambulance came along to collect the woman. My dad watched as they loaded her onto the stretcher, not willing to leave the scene until the ambulance had closed the doors and whisked her safely away. Not only was it the *right* thing to do, it was the *kind* thing to do. Dad noticed a woman who had obviously encountered some hard living, and he wouldn't turn away.

Too many people look away, figuratively walking over the body of a hurting person. What if we taught our kids to stop and see the people around them, to notice others, and to act with kindness? What if we encouraged our kids to reach out to the lonely child on the playground or the one who doesn't fit in? What if kindness became their operating principle? Think of the changes that could take place in our world if kindness became common among us.

So the first reason to intentionally encourage kindness is that our world needs it so much.

Another good reason to encourage kindness is that God commands it. Ephesians 4:32 is well known, but do we really follow its command? "Be kind to one another, tenderhearted, forgiving one another, as God in Christ forgave you."

The words *kind*, *tenderhearted*, and *forgiving* all have the idea of graciousness and compassion behind them. These are not self-focused ideas, but rather, they focus on bestowing goodness on others, just as Jesus did throughout the Gospels. I realize as I read this verse and try to live it out in my life that none of this is easy.

Further, notice that being kind, tenderhearted, and forgiving is not a mere suggestion. There is no exception for people who are hard to get along with or people we simply don't like. This verse doesn't say we can withhold kindness from certain family members, not even the especially difficult ones. No, this is a command, and God didn't simply give the command for the sake of giving a command—he gave us the reason too. Why be kind, tenderhearted, and forgiving? Because Jesus Christ led the way and did the same for us first.

> **When we show kindness to others . . . we model the grace that Jesus came to bring.**

Finally, I think one of the most compelling reasons for us to show kindness is rooted in Christ and the gospel: to bring others to repentance and redemption. Romans 2:4 says: "Don't you see how wonderfully kind, tolerant, and patient God is with you? Does this mean nothing to you? Can't you see that his kindness is intended to turn you from your sin?" (NLT). Or, as the English Standard Version puts it, "God's kindness is meant to lead you to repentance."

You see, kindness is undeserved; it cannot be demanded. Kindness is an act of grace. When we show kindness to others, when we sacrifice our own comfort for the sake of another, when we really see the pain of another person, we model the grace that Jesus came to bring. And it is that grace that leads us to repentance.

God's work through Christ Jesus on the cross, the greatest sacrifice ever made, is the ultimate act of kindness. We are to see the kindness of Jesus as a call to put aside our differences, to put aside our preferences, and to see our own deep need of a Savior. God's kindness demands a heart change.

A Cup of Water Could Make All the Difference

Too many people today have bought into the world's lie that kindness doesn't matter. Perhaps you've even stopped noticing others, or doing for others, because you think your actions won't make a difference. Let's stop and take a look at Jesus. In John 4, we read of one of the kindest things Jesus ever did when he was on earth—he asked for a drink of water.

Jesus and his disciples had been traveling, walking great distances each day to bring good news to hurting people (a kindness in itself). One particularly hot and dusty day, Jesus sits down at a well alone, waiting for his disciples to come back with some food. Soon, Scripture tells us, a Samaritan woman comes to draw water—in the heat of the day!—and Jesus asks her for a drink.

Just a simple request for a drink of water, but Jesus's kindness here is life changing. You see, Jews did not acknowledge Samaritans. In fact, most Jews would rather crawl another mile on their hands and knees over dusty, dirty roads to find another well before they would ask a Samaritan for a drink of water. For Jesus to ask for, and then accept, a drink from this woman was unusually kind.

His request surprises her! At first she objects, asking Jesus why he would even bother to ask her for water since she was well aware of how Jews felt about people like her. But she draws the water anyway and gives him a drink, which he humbly accepts.

That isn't the end of the encounter, though. Jesus stays and talks to the woman, even asks her questions about her life and tells her things about herself that any ordinary man would not know. He knows her background—that she has had five husbands and that she isn't married to the man she is living with now. He knows that she has not lived a pure and holy life.

Jesus noticed the Samaritan woman. He noticed her pain. He noticed that she was an outcast (who else would draw water at noon?). He noticed that she didn't necessarily want to live the life she had lived, yet this was her lot, maybe because she needed protection or comfort from a man. Jesus noticed everything about this woman, and still he asked her for water.

And in his kindness, Jesus offers her something that only he could give—life. He talks to her about her life and about a better life, an eternal life. And he offers her "water" of his own that will satisfy her forever. Very quickly, the woman knows that she has met the Messiah; she leaves her water jar at the well and runs to tell the rest of her village: "He told me everything I ever did!" (John 4:39 NLT). And, the Bible tells us, many in her village believed in Jesus as well.

What was the result of Jesus's kindness? For perhaps the first time in her life, this woman felt important, seen, known, and as a result, she believed that Jesus was who he said he was. "Can this be the Christ?" she asked (John 4:29). And it all started with a simple drink of water.

What if we took notice? What if we taught our kids to notice? What if we humbled ourselves and took the time to talk to someone who feels outcast or different? Jesus did it. Can we?

A Word About Sibling Rivalry

Right about now you're probably thinking, *That's great, Shelly. Those are lofty goals—being more like Jesus, asking people for help, showing kindness to strangers—but I can't even get my kids to be kind to one another!*

I feel your pain. Every parent who has had more than one child has dealt with sibling rivalry. And every parent has had to decide whether to let it go because it's just what siblings do or to stop it in its tracks. I think this is probably one of the most challenging parts of our job.

Our sinful nature causes us to be unkind, which especially seems to manifest itself in sibling relationships. But sibling rivalry, fighting, bickering, whatever you want to call it, doesn't have to have the last word in our families. If we are serious about practicing intentional discipleship, we will see our homes as the training ground where we teach our kids how to treat others. If we want our children to be kind, we have to train them to be kind to the people it's hardest to be kind to—their siblings.

I love these words from C. S. Lewis: "Do not waste time bothering whether you 'love' your neighbor; act as if you did."[4] In our homes this is especially important. When we teach our kids to act in a loving way toward their siblings, when we insist on kindness rather than simply accepting sibling rivalry as a normal part of growing up, we teach them to love those who may be hardest to love.

Of course we see the flaws in our family members more acutely than in people we don't know as well. Of course we know the weaknesses of those under our roofs. It's tempting to use these flaws and weaknesses against our family members, and sometimes we do, but parents, I want to urge you to stop this type of behavior right now. Today. Oh, it won't be easy, and it probably won't look perfect, but it will be worth it because the growing harmony in your home (OK, the *attempt* at harmony) may just be the light, that cup of cold water, that others need to see.

Listen, I know it's tough enough to get your kids to get along, let alone act in kind ways toward one another. Figuring out the best way for your family to change old habits may take some time and creative parenting, but you can do it, as long as you are convinced, like me, that a little kindness goes a long way.

Here are a few ideas for intentionally training your kids to be kind. First, catch them in the act of kindness. Encourage them by telling them that you saw how Janie offered Johnny the first piece of gum out of the package or how Sam shared his toys with his younger sister. Encouraging kindness goes a long way toward instilling this habit.

Second, talk about examples of kindness when you see them. Use the word *kind* rather than the word *nice*, and talk about the difference between the two. Share examples of kindness, such as the fifth-grade boys from Minnesota who came alongside their classmate James. Explain that friendships are born out of kindness.

Third, encourage your child to "see the need" and act accordingly. Simple acts like holding the door for another person, emptying the dishwasher, or taking out the trash without being asked may later lead to more courageous acts of kindness such as that of Travis Rudolph. May our children have eyes that are open to the needs around them.

Talk about examples of kindness when you see them.

In her best-selling book *Wonder,* author R. J. Palacio creates a beloved character, Mr. Browne, a fifth-grade teacher. Mr. Browne begins the school year by sharing some classroom rules about "really important things." His main rule? "When given the choice between being right and being kind, choose kind."[5] Now, this teacher isn't talking about finding ultimate truth here—he's talking about our inherent need to be right or to win an argument, which often leads to unkindness. I think this may be a good rule for all of us, not just fifth graders. Maybe if we took our focus off ourselves (being right) and focused on others (being kind), our world would be a much better place.

Kindness starts right where we are—in our homes, in our neighborhoods, in our classrooms, and yes, even (or perhaps *especially*) in our churches. And it starts because of the kindness of Christ that has been extended to each one of us.

Wouldn't it be great if the kids in your neighborhood found refuge in your home simply because of the kindness they see there? Wouldn't it be wonderful if the kids at school thought of our children not as the "athlete" or the "actress" or the "academic," but instead saw our child as kind? Because if we're into labeling people, that's the label I would choose for my child. And wouldn't it be amazing if those in our community were drawn to our church because its members reflected the kindness of Jesus?

Let's raise kids who excel in kindness. Let's raise kids who take notice of others—the lonely, the outcast, the hurting—and share kindness with them. That way others will see Jesus in them and be drawn to the kindness of the Father.

Consider

1. Why is kindness important? Is it important to include this in your family's travel plan? Why or why not?
2. What is one way you have intentionally practiced kindness toward your family this week? What are some practical steps you can take to help your children act kindly toward one another?
3. Read John 4. List some of the ways Jesus showed kindness to the Samaritan woman. What was the result of Jesus's kindness to this woman (v. 39)? How can your family extend kindness to others? List some goals or steps you can take in this area.

HEART WORK

Intentional Service

SNOW STARTED FLYING IN THE LATE AFTERNOON, AND BY DINNER-time my dad was pulling on his boots and warmest jacket. As the snow quickly accumulated, we knew it would be a long night for Dad, who, during the winter months, served as our township road commissioner. That meant he was the person responsible for clearing the drifting snow off the many miles of country roads in our area.

Sometime in the middle of the night I was awakened by voices downstairs, so I threw on a sweater and headed toward the noise, thinking it must certainly be my dad who had come in to warm up. I smelled coffee and grinned—my parents could drink coffee at any time of the day or night. It was their sustenance.

As I crept down the stairs, however, I heard a man's voice that I didn't recognize. Sitting at the kitchen table with a coffee cup in his hand was a man I had never seen before. My mom stood nervously next to the kitchen counter as she offered him something to eat.

"No thanks. Coffee's fine," I heard the stranger say.

"What's going on?" I asked as I entered the kitchen.

Mom explained that Jerry's car had gotten stuck in the ditch just down the road from our house. This was long before the days of cell phones, so the two were just waiting together in the kitchen until Dad came back.

"Shouldn't be long," she said, and told me to go back to bed.

The next morning the blizzard had ended, and Dad sat at the kitchen table, drinking coffee, of course, after a full night of plowing the roads. Mom was still in the kitchen and looked like she hadn't gotten any sleep either. Jerry's car was now out of the ditch—Dad had come to the rescue with chains and the snow plow sometime during the night. What I didn't know earlier, however, was that Jerry was drunk when his car careened off the snow-packed road. Because ours was the closest house, he knocked on our door for refuge and, thanks to the coffee, eventually sobered up.

"Mom! That could have been dangerous!" I protested when I learned the full story. But Mom insisted that he was harmless—just an old man in our neighborhood who had fallen on hard times. What else could she do but let him in during a snowstorm?

I still remember that night because it taught me so much about service, which is something my parents modeled so well. Dad served our community in many ways, even when it wasn't convenient, like when it required him to drive a snowplow all night. And Mom also served even when it felt uncomfortable. She opened her home to those who needed help or a place to stay, even to a drunk man who had come pounding on our door.

I watched my parents carefully when I was growing up—what kid doesn't, right?—and I noticed their acts of service, both in our church and in our community. Once I asked my mom why she volunteered so much, and her answer has remained with me to this day. She simply said, "If there is a need and I can fill it, I'll do it." How very different from the not-my-job mentality we so often see today.

"If there is a need and I can fill it, I'll do it." This doesn't mean that my parents ran around doing everything; they had plenty of time for family and work. But it did mean that they were open and willing to serve, and in so doing modeled a life poured out for others. They showed me in big and small ways that our service matters—to God, to others, and to our children.

What Is Biblical Servanthood?

Did you know that the word *service* (or *serve*) is mentioned over four hundred times in the Bible? Four hundred! That's a lot of mentions. And even more startling, the word *servant* is used over nine hundred times.

This tells me that service must be important to God. But, we might ask, why?

In the book of Matthew, chapter 20, we find Jesus and his disciples pulling away from the massive crowds that followed him everywhere. Jesus had been privately telling the Twelve exactly what was going to happen to him in order to prepare them for his death, burial, and resurrection. As the following verses make clear, however, the disciples didn't fully understand what Jesus meant:

> Then the mother of the sons of Zebedee came up to him with her sons, and kneeling before him she asked him for something. And he said to her, "What do you want?" She said to him, "Say that these two sons of mine are to sit, one at your right hand and one at your left, in your kingdom." Jesus answered, "You do not know what you are asking. Are you able to drink the cup that I am to drink? . . .
>
> "Whoever would be great among you must be your servant, and whoever would be first among you must be your slave, even as the Son of Man came not to be served but to serve, and to give his life as a ransom for many." (vv. 20–22, 26–28)

Let's set the scene. Here we have two of Jesus's disciples, James and John, along with their mother (never a good sign when the mother gets involved!), who want to have a chat with him. Mother Zebedee asks for an incredible favor from Jesus once he's the king—could her two sons please sit on either side of him? It's clear that they don't understand the nature of Christ's kingdom.

Jesus knows that this request isn't really coming from their mother, so he addresses James and John directly. He tells them they don't have a clue what they're asking for. The cup of suffering that Jesus was about to drink was going to be a bitter cup—one that they would never ask for if they fully understood the implications of it. Their question, according to Jesus, was naive.

Furthermore, their request stirred up conflict among the other ten disciples. *What does this mean for us, then?* they wondered. *We want to rule with Jesus too.* Now we see that none of the twelve disciples understood that being a ruler, someone in authority, isn't about place or privilege. It's about service.

Jesus quickly drives his point home when he tells them how a leader should really act: "But whoever would be great among you must be your servant, and whoever would be first among you must be your slave" (Matt. 20:26–27). *Servant. Slave.* These words make us cringe, and maybe that's exactly why Jesus used them. But perhaps he wanted his disciples to see that there is nothing about being a king, a leader, a ruler that is special. The special ones are the servants.

Jesus has been revealing the facts about himself to the disciples all along, but now he tells them clearly why he has come—and it's not to be a king. Even though Jesus had all authority in heaven and on earth, he reminds the disciples of his calling: "The Son of Man came not to be served but to serve, and to give his life as a ransom for many" (Matt. 20:28). And, indeed, it was on the cross that Jesus, the suffering servant, was fully exalted.

If we want to know what a servant looks like, we need to look at Jesus. Servants don't seek honor or fame or glory; servants pour out their lives for others.

Here's the wonderful thing about Jesus. His service, although it would result in his death, was not drudgery to him. Hebrews 12:2 tells us that Jesus endured the torture of the cross "for the joy that was set before him." Christ had the proper perspective about serving—yes, it required that he sacrifice, pour himself out, but the anticipation of being reunited with his Father in heaven and bringing salvation to earth also brought him great joy. He did not focus on the act of service itself but on the reward that lay ahead of him.

What about you? Do your children see your willingness to serve wholeheartedly, joyfully, for the cause of Christ? Or do they see you seeking honor and recognition? If serving others has become a chore, you might need to make some changes, starting with gaining a proper perspective on what service is and what service is not.

What Service Is Not

First, service is not always easy. Yes, there are times when serving feels easy, joyful, and fun—those times are great. We all want to serve where we feel our gifts are being used well, but sometimes service feels like a great deal of sacrifice. With Jesus, the Suffering Servant, as our model, we know that's exactly what it is.

Our friend Daniel started an after-school ministry to teenagers in one of the most dangerous, poverty-stricken neighborhoods in Chicago. He runs a house where teens can hang out after school, a safe place where they can talk, do homework, or just stay off the streets.

Daniel's work hours aren't the usual nine to five. He wants to be there for the kids after school, so he often doesn't get home to his family until later in the evening. Over the years Daniel has lost many friends to violence, a sadness he carries with him every day. His days are long and tiring, and the kids he talks with are dealing with heavy issues. Is this work easy? Absolutely not. But Daniel keeps going because he knows God loves those kids, and Daniel feels called to show them that love.

> **Sometimes service feels like a great deal of sacrifice.**

Second, service is not always convenient. Emergencies happen at unexpected times: people get sick; families need meals; a neighbor needs to talk when we're late for a meeting. Sometimes we are called to meet the needs of people who are not like us at all, which can feel a little uncomfortable. Other times we're called to serve those closest to us, even if it's inconvenient.

My friend Holly helped her in-laws move from their home several states away so that they could be closer to family. She spent weeks packing their belongings, cleaning out their home to get it ready to sell, and eventually, settling them into a new home. Once they were closer, Holly spent most mornings checking on her in-laws and running errands for them.

One day, Holly's young daughter, who had been watching her mother's hard work for weeks on end, asked an innocent question: "Mom, are you getting paid for all this?" Holly just laughed and said no, she wasn't getting paid. It was a great opportunity to explain to her daughter that even though service is inconvenient at times, we do it because we love Jesus and we love our family. Holly understood *why* she sacrificed, and her service gave her an opportunity to pass that intention on to her daughter.

Finally, service is never, ever about me. Oh, there are times I wish it were—days when I want people to recognize the sacrifice I've made to bring a meal or to serve the homeless (such small things, really). But then Scripture reminds me of Jesus's example: "In your relationships with one another, have the same mindset as Christ Jesus: Who, being in very nature God, did not consider equality with God something to be used to his own advantage; rather, he made himself nothing by taking the very nature of a servant" (Phil. 2:5–7 NIV).

Think about it—Jesus is God. His very nature is divine. If anyone had a reason to seek fame or glory, it was Jesus, yet he took on human form so that he could come to earth to serve, sacrificially, so others would live. He gave everything he had for a world that was desperately lost.

Scripture reminds me that when I seek recognition, I'm seeking the wrong thing.

Jesus knew his purpose—to obey God to the point of death on a cross (Phil. 2:8). We all, including our children, also have a purpose during our time on earth. When we serve, we show our children that our purpose—and theirs—is to serve others, not ourselves, to the glory of God. Jesus served, not to gain credit, but to glorify God, and so should we.

Why Serve?

If service is hard, inconvenient, and sacrificial, why should we teach our kids to live this way? At first glance, service certainly doesn't seem like the pathway to joy, does it? But as those who follow Jesus know, his ways don't always make sense here on this earth. Some describe this as an "upside-down" kingdom. Just as Philippians 2 explains, Jesus's model may seem upside down, but it's the model that teaches us that service matters.

First, our service matters to God. As I've noted, God's Word talks about service and servanthood a lot (nine hundred times, remember?), so servanthood obviously matters to him. But it's not enough to just hear the words "Be a servant." We must teach our children to obey them.

James 1:22–25 says this: "Don't just listen to God's word. You must do what it says. Otherwise, you are only fooling yourselves. For if you listen to the word and don't obey, it is like glancing at your face in a mirror. You see yourself, walk away, and forget what you look like. But if you look carefully into the perfect law that sets you free, and if you do what it says and don't forget what you heard, then God will bless you for doing it" (NLT).

Parents, teaching our kids God's Word isn't enough. (I know that sounds like heresy, but hear me out.) We have to be willing to get out there and actually do what it says, even if it's uncomfortable, even if it requires some sacrifice on our part. Because when we teach our children the value of servanthood we are actually obeying God, and our obedience matters to him.

Second, our service matters to others. This may seem obvious—when we help someone else, when we make ourselves available to others, it makes a difference. James drives this point home when he says, "What good is it, dear brothers and sisters, if you say you have faith but don't show it by your actions? Can that kind of faith save anyone? Suppose you see a brother or sister who has no food or clothing, and you say, 'Good-bye and have a good day; stay warm and eat well'—but then you don't give that person any food or clothing. What good does that do?" (James 2:14–16 NLT).

What good, indeed? The Bible is clear: if we have real faith, we will serve others. Period. If as parents we would demonstrate what genuine faith looks like, we will prioritize service and meet the needs of others around us to the best of our ability.

Several families in our church have made serving the homeless a priority. These families faithfully show up at our local homeless shelter, make beds, serve food, and talk to the guests. Children as young as three or four years old joyfully help their parents arrange sheets on the beds and lovingly serve food to the hungry and the hurting. These children are learning early in life that followers of Jesus are people who serve. And their service matters.

Finally, our service matters to our own hearts. When we serve, our focus becomes clearer, and our eyes become trained not on our own needs or problems but on the needs and problems of others. And this focus gives us (and our kids) a good dose of perspective. Craving a bigger house? Try serving in a homeless ministry, and you'll be more grateful for that roof over your head, no matter how big or how small. Wishing for a different career or a better job? Try volunteering with the unemployed, and you'll be glad to get up to go to work in the mornings.

While serving others should not be about our receiving kudos or recognition, there are some intrinsic rewards that tend to occur. A survey of college students revealed that those who volunteered in some capacity realized greater personal growth and maturity than students who did not. One student remarked, "It [volunteering] can help you with your own personal problems to see that there are people whose problems are a lot worse. . . . I mean, teenagers often do a lot of emoting about things that shrink down to size when you see the bigger, more serious things other people have to deal with."[1] It seems natural to conclude, then, that college students who develop empathy will likely become more empathetic adults.

Richard Foster says in *Celebration of Discipline*, "In service we must experience the many little deaths of going beyond ourselves. Service banishes us to the mundane, the ordinary, the trivial."[2] I don't know about you, but I want my children to have eyes that see past themselves to the grieving, the hurting, the broken. I want my children to die to themselves for the sake of others. We may be tempted to think of our service as mundane or trivial, but I believe with all my heart that serving others is the antidote to self-centered living and the pathway toward a more grateful heart. We must intentionally model servanthood for our kids.

Models of Service

Our friends Roger and Becky are in their sixties, but they sure don't act like it! Always up for an adventure, they have modeled a life of faithful service for their four children, two of whom are serving in overseas ministry, sometimes in very dangerous places. Roger and Becky have joyfully served the members of our church for many years—if you know them, you know they are always smiling. But they had never served overseas until recently, when they had an opportunity to lead a team to the Greek island of Lesvos in the Aegean Sea, just a few miles off the coast of Turkey, to work in a refugee camp for about ten days. They shared with Brian and me that they were nervous about taking this trip because of their age and their lack of experience working with refugees. They said, "We weren't sure we should be the ones to go." But God called them to serve, so they went.

After their trip the four of us had dinner together, and Roger's and Becky's gratitude for their experience was clear as they shared about family after family they had met, refugees who had fled the dangers of their home countries with nothing but the clothes on their backs. Our friends were bursting with stories about the people they had grown to love in such a short time and the burden they now carried for refugees. God had worked on their hearts—so much so that they signed up for a second short-term trip to Greece to serve refugees.

Rather than feel sad or defeated about the scope of the refugee problem in Greece, Roger and Becky exhibited an irrepressible joy. They had seen God at work in the camp. Despite the horrible, overcrowded conditions, people had hope. And people were being cared for in the name of Jesus. Because of their experience, our friends understood in a new way that a life of serving others brings tremendous joy. They took a risk, obeyed God's call, and stepped out to serve.

What would the world look like if people didn't serve others? There would be no safe places for refugees. There would be no homeless shelters. There would be no food banks or safe houses in dangerous neighborhoods or any other of the millions of ways people serve others.

But not just that. We would limit or eliminate one vehicle God uses to grow us to be more like him. When we serve, and when our kids serve alongside us, we see God's compassionate heart for all people, and we gain the opportunity to practice sharing it with others. Jesus came to serve *everyone*, not just those who are pretty and smell nice and speak our language. Everyone. And we should serve likewise.

Jesus provided an example of service that surprised his disciples the night before his crucifixion—he knelt in front of them to wash their dirty feet (John 13:1–17). Maybe that was his way of intentionally discipling his followers one last time by modeling what it means to be a servant. He knew what would happen the next day and two days after that, even if his disciples didn't really get it. And yet his focus wasn't on the suffering ahead but on taking a towel, kneeling low, and serving his followers. Still teaching until his very last hour.

And, ultimately, his sacrificial service made all the difference.

Consider

1. Why is service important? Is it important to include this in your family's travel plan? Why or why not?

2. How have you encouraged your children (or how can you encourage them) to serve other members of the family? Have you seen a change of heart because of that service?

3. What is one way you enjoy serving others as a family? With your kids, make a list of ways that you can actively love your neighbors. Here are some ideas you might include: cut the grass of an elderly neighbor, blow the snow off the sidewalks on your entire block rather than just your little section, bake cookies for the new family down the street, adopt a refugee family in your community, or volunteer in a local homeless shelter.

9

MONEY MATTERS

Intentional Stewardship

I'M WHAT SOME WOULD CALL A RIGHT-BRAINED WOMAN. I LOVE thinking about ideas, solving problems creatively, and helping my students learn new concepts. My husband is a predominately left-brained guy—he enjoys strategizing, planning, and, yes, thinking about finances. Much to my husband's chagrin, I have zero interest in learning about money; in fact, I can barely even balance my checkbook. It's a sad state of affairs, really, and not one I recommend. I have given thanks to the Lord more times than I can count that I married a finance expert, because I'm fairly certain that without Brian's guidance I would be in a lot of trouble.

Ours is an interesting partnership, but lest you think that, because he works in finance, my husband's a curmudgeon about money, always checking my receipts and questioning my spending habits, I'm here to tell you that's not the case. In fact, we rarely, if ever, disagree about money. And here's why: we have learned to respect each other in this area. He's generous with me when I need to spend money, and I'm on board (grateful, even) with his saving habits. It works out.

But I know our relationship is unusual. In fact, according to the American Academy of Matrimonial Lawyers, differing opinions about how to handle money is one of the main reasons marriages fall apart.[1] Most American adults don't have a good grasp on how to handle money, and that lack of knowledge is affecting their children. Very soon, if we haven't already reached this point, we will live in a nation that is clueless about finances.

Unfortunately, those who know very little about handling finances are often the very ones who are being entrusted with credit. Today's college students are bombarded with credit card offers—just because they are in college! That seems a little crazy to me, especially since today's research shows that most college students (84 percent) have at least one credit card and an average debt on those cards of $3,173.[2] Studies also show that carrying over a balance of more than one thousand dollars on a credit card is considered risky for college students, and that debt load has been associated with behaviors such as drug and alcohol abuse.[3] Furthermore, students who leave college with credit card debt are likely to become adults who also have trouble with debt.[4]

> **We must discuss stewardship, the God-honoring use of our time and resources, including money.**

As we disciple our children, we must discuss stewardship, the God-honoring use of our time and resources, including money. Mom and Dad, these are critical discussions because research shows the best place for our kids to learn about money is from their parents.[5] In fact, college students who remember having conversations about money with their parents generally have greater financial knowledge than their peers and have fewer financial problems later in life. Also, students whose parents frequently argued about money have higher credit card debt than those whose parents did not argue about money.[6]

We must help our children become masters of their money before money masters them.

What Is Stewardship?

When Julia was born, some friends gave us a baby blanket as a gift. It was pretty basic—just a simple polyester blanket, pink and white, but it was soft. Oh, so soft. And it was just the right size to cover an infant and just the right size and weight to be carried around by a toddler. Which Julia did.

Remember the character Linus in the old *Peanuts* cartoons? Linus dragged his blanket around everywhere he went, even into his most famous scene in *A Charlie Brown Christmas*. That was my Julia. Every night she slept with her "Blankie," as she called it, until Blankie was reduced to a tattered shred of fabric.

Julia loved her Blankie. She was totally attached to her Blankie. Wherever Julia was, you could be sure that Blankie was never far away, and if, by some chance, Blankie got left somewhere, she would get a panicked look in her eyes and say, "Where's Blankie?" At dinnertime, I'd often have to put my foot down and tell Julia that Blankie was not, in fact, going to eat dinner with us (it smelled pretty bad sometimes), but that Blankie would wait in the living room until dinner was over.

Bedtime was the worst because Julia could not sleep without Blankie, and, true story, Blankie always had to be cold—as in, we had to put it in the freezer for a few minutes before bedtime so that the blanket was cold to the touch when Julia settled down to sleep.

Crazy, I know.

But Julia loved Blankie. So much so that at times she treated it like a pet! Blankie was her security and her treasure; she was never far from it. But when she grew up, like, say, closer to kindergarten age, she had to give up her Blankie. She couldn't remain attached to it forever, so we went through the difficult process of extricating Blankie from Julia's grip and from her heart.

I realize that this is a simplistic illustration of a much bigger concept, but I think it works. Julia's Blankie was her treasure; it was something her heart longed for. But as she grew up, she had to release her attachment to it. It's the same with us regarding money. As we grow closer to Jesus, we cannot continue to love our money or the things of this world the way we once did. Scripture tells us plainly in Matthew 6:21, "Where your treasure is, there your heart will be also."

Stewardship is a matter of the heart.

Why Stewardship?

Where is your treasure? What do you value? What consumes your thoughts? Our values and thoughts point to our heart's treasure—in other words, what we love. Jesus tells us plainly that if our treasure is here on earth, we cannot love God: "You cannot serve God and money" (Matt. 6:24).

And this is the first reason we must, early on, teach our kids a proper perspective toward money. Because if money is our child's treasure, they will not grow in their love for God. Neither will *we* grow deeper in love with God if we treasure money; we simply cannot. So when we talk about money issues, we're also talking about heart health. We must teach our children to treasure the right things so that their hearts will grow strong, their roots will grow deep, and their faith will last.

As Matthew Henry, the great Bible commentator, said, "The heart is God's due (Prov. 23:26), and that he may have it, our treasure must be laid up with him, and then our souls will be lifted up to him."[7] God deserves our first and foremost loyalty. He should be our first desire, and as we grow in him, the things of this world, particularly money, will have diminishing control over us. I want my children to love God above all else, and I'm pretty sure you want the same for your kids.

Second, I never want my children to buy into the mistaken notion that what they have has anything to do with what they've done, so I take care to disciple them in the area of stewardship. I want them to enjoy a life that, as Jesus put it, is truly life, abundant life (John 10:10), so I teach my children that we have a responsibility to God for the gifts he's given to us, not just financially but in every way—our time, our resources, our minds, our homes. *Everything* we have is God's; we are merely caretakers of these gifts. A proper perspective allows us to steward our finances and all our gifts well and in a way that honors God.

Jesus or Money? A Biblical Understanding of the Good Life

The Bible tells the story of a rich young man—the Bible calls him a "ruler," someone who was in authority—who was looking for that abundant life. Mark 10:17–22 summarizes this encounter:

As he was setting out on his journey, a man ran up and knelt before him and asked him, "Good Teacher, what must I do to inherit eternal life?" And Jesus said to him, "Why do you call me good? No one is good except God alone. You know the commandments: 'Do not murder, Do not commit adultery, Do not steal, Do not bear false witness, Do not defraud, Honor your father and mother.'" And he said to him, "Teacher, all these I have kept from my youth." And Jesus, looking at him, loved him, and said to him, "You lack one thing: go, sell all that you have and give to the poor, and you will have treasure in heaven; and come, follow me." Disheartened by the saying, he went away sorrowful, for he had great possessions.

Jesus had been teaching all day and was just heading out to another location (v. 17). We can assume that the young man had been listening to Jesus as he taught; maybe he had been holding back, waiting for just the right moment to speak up, but when he saw that he might lose his chance, he "ran up and knelt before him." He desperately wanted an answer to the question that had been burning in his chest all day: "What must I do to inherit eternal life?" This is the most important question in the world! The one many people still want to know the answer to, even today. Eternal life is of utmost importance, and this young man knew it.

I think, however, that the rich young ruler wanted Jesus to give him a list of things he could *do*—something like, go wash your face and hands and set the table for dinner and everything will be fine. And it looks like Jesus is heading in that direction at first as he lists off the first five of the Ten Commandments, those that deal with our relationships with others.

This is going to be easy! the ruler must have been thinking, because, as he tells Jesus, he's kept all those commandments. Jesus already knows he thinks this because he knows the young man's heart; Jesus knows exactly where this man's treasure is.

Interestingly, Jesus does not mention the last five of the Ten Commandments, those that deal with our relationship to God. He does this intentionally, because Jesus understands that, while this may be a "good" person whose horizontal relationships are in order, his heart, and therefore his worship, is not directed toward God; his treasure is somewhere else.

I love how Mark's version of this story adds one little detail that the other gospel accounts do not: "And Jesus, looking at him, loved him" (v. 21). Remember the chapter about kindness, where I said that kindness was really looking, really seeing someone? That's what's happening here. Jesus is so kind to this man. He sees him, he knows his heart is divided, and still he loves him. He truly loves him. Jesus knows that this man is hungry for answers to questions of eternal significance, and he shows great compassion before he asks this man to reveal his heart.

"Go, sell all that you have and give to the poor" (v. 21). Bam! Jesus goes for the jugular. He asks him to do the very thing that, for this man, is impossible because he loves his stuff too much. Now, please understand this: selling everything we have and giving it to the poor is *not* a requirement for salvation. Jesus is calling this man to do this thing because he knows where his heart is—that it is full of idolatry, that he loves his money more than he loves Jesus.

The encounter ends very quickly after that. The Bible tells us that the man goes away sad. I think Jesus goes away sad too because this young ruler, whom he loves, cannot do what is required of him. He cannot give away all that he owns because his heart is too tied up in his possessions. His treasure is here on earth—in his house, his chariots, his clothes. It's just too much to ask that he give it all away for Jesus—even to gain eternal life.

> **Your bank statement says more about your heart than anything.**

And here's where I have to ask myself: what am I modeling for my kids, especially when it comes to how I handle my finances? Am I like the rich young ruler who cannot even think about giving up everything for Jesus? Am I holding anything back, thinking that I've earned it or deserve it? What does my treasure reveal about my heart? As my husband always tells our girls: "Your bank statement says more about your heart than anything."

Financial Principles to Live By

The story of the rich young ruler challenges and convicts me. I don't want to fall prey to the trap of riches. The rich man loved money so much it became an idol to him, so I must ask myself, what do I love more than Jesus? If it's money (actually, if it's *anything*), I must make some changes. This story challenges me to teach my children how to handle their own finances so that money will not become a vice to them. They also need to understand that money is a tool, and, if handled correctly, it can be used for much good in their lives and in the lives of others.

Early on, Brian and I set out to teach our daughters some financial principles, based on the Bible's teaching about money.

The first principle is fairly simple but challenging: what we have is not ours—we are merely stewards of the gifts God has given us. A steward is someone who manages the property of another; in this case, we who follow Jesus manage the many gifts, both spiritual and material, that we've been given. In 1 Corinthians 12, we read that God has given spiritual gifts to each one of us. These gifts differ in responsibility and reach, but they are all to be used for the common good (v. 7), to build up the church and its members, because if one member of the body suffers, everyone suffers (v. 26).

How does this relate to money? It's fairly simple. We've all been given an amount of money to use in helping others. In fact, we have a *responsibility* to help those in need, and I think we'd all agree that the world is in desperate need right now. Some of us have more money than others, but let's face it, if we live in America, we have more; we are some of the wealthiest people on the planet.

You may be completely baffled as to how you can follow God's command to help others if you can barely buy groceries for your family. You are not alone. Research tells us that nearly 50 percent of Americans are now living paycheck to paycheck, meaning they would be unable to come up with four hundred dollars to cover an emergency, and more than 60 percent of us do not have a thousand dollars in savings.[8] These statistics alone should wake us up and motivate us to get our financial houses in order. As stewards, we are called to accountability and wisdom when it comes to handling our finances; no matter what our means, we can look for ways to help others.

The second principle we've stressed with our daughters is that money should never be our master. Just as the rich young ruler did, we will fall under the power of money if we love the things of this world too much. So we've always taught our girls to live below their means, to stay out of debt, and to keep their hearts tied to Jesus, not to worldly riches.

That's not to say we need to live monastic lifestyles, never buying anything for ourselves and giving every penny away. Some are called to that ascetic lifestyle, but that calling, I think, is rare. No, God doesn't always call us to suffer financially, but he does always call us to be accountable for how we manage the gifts he's given us. We need to ask ourselves what is driving the decisions we make about the way we spend our money if we hope to be accountable to God.

The third guiding principle we have taught our children is that money is a tool for building the kingdom of God, and if we're giving money to the kingdom, generosity should always be our goal. This, I think, is where teaching our kids about money becomes fun because when we give our money away, we find true joy. The Bible is loaded with truth regarding this principle.

Take, for instance, Proverbs 11:25, which says, "Whoever brings blessing will be enriched, and one who waters will himself be watered." God promises refreshment when we refresh others through our giving. Or Proverbs 3:9–10: "Honor the LORD with your wealth and with the firstfruits of all your produce; then your barns will be filled with plenty, and your vats will be bursting with wine." God gives and gives and gives some more, so we should do the same and use his gifts to help others. He promises to replenish our supply so that we can continue to do good.

Let me be clear, however: this is not the "prosperity gospel," as some call it. God's principle is not that we should give away so that we can get more for ourselves. God wants us to give generously so that we can continue to give to others. If we are faithful with the little God has given us, he will give us responsibility for helping others in even bigger ways. A generous person is one God can trust with more responsibility, so as we give generously, he will continue to provide opportunities to give even more.

I married a generous man. Brian loves nothing more than helping others with our resources—it's one of his spiritual gifts—and he wants to pass this passion on to our daughters. We believe that God commands us to tithe, to give at least 10 percent of our income back to him, so we wanted our girls to get in the habit of tithing early in their lives. (I'll talk more about how we handled finances later.) But as our girls grew older, we continued to train them to give. *Where* we give our money is as important as how much we give because, again, we are called to be responsible stewards. We believe that God wants us first to support our local church, but we also support other organizations that help the poor and spread the gospel.

Recently, Brian and I called a family meeting and talked openly with our young adult daughters about our giving. Now that they are older and making giving decisions of their own, we thought that practicing these principles was in order. We shared a list of charities we've supported over the past few years and told our daughters exactly how much we've given away. We talked to them about *why* we give to the organizations we support. We then allotted each girl a small portion of our giving budget for the year and told them that we would follow up in six months. During those months, each girl was to think carefully about what they're passionate about, research some possible charities that they would like to support, pray about what God might want them to do, and then make a presentation to the rest of the family regarding the rationale for their gift.

Yes, it sounds like a lot of work, but when we act as stewards who manage God's money, when we commit to mastering our money, and when our goal is generosity, some work is required. Our girls came through just like I knew they would—each one presented a carefully thought-out plan for the money they were responsible for, and our entire family grew in our joy of giving.

Starting Our Kids on the Road to
Intentional Stewardship

Because so many people have asked Brian and me how we taught our kids about money, I thought I would share some ideas with you. These ideas were based partly on how I was raised—my parents put me on a clothing allowance in high school, and it taught me so much—and partly on the principles above. Our goal was to intentionally teach our girls to give generously, save carefully, and spend with joy and thanksgiving.

When each child turned four years old, we started training her by giving her four quarters every Saturday night. Saturday night was a strategic choice because one of the quarters would be needed the next day at church. Each child had three jars labeled "God," "Save," and "Spend." (You may have heard of the jar idea before—we weren't out to reinvent the wheel here!) As money was dropped into each jar, we'd recite, "One for God, one for saving, two for spending." Please notice that the God jar was *always* first—we did this intentionally because we truly believe that God should get his portion first, no matter what, and this was the beginning of that training for our girls.

As the girls got older, their allowance grew—first four quarters, then eight (we'd recite the little saying twice just to reinforce the idea), then four one-dollar bills. Once they reached junior high (they were long past the three jars by then), we'd give them a little more money. But we always expected them to give a portion back to God and to save a portion before they spent anything on themselves.

A few years later, we felt that our daughters should take some responsibility for paying for the things they wanted—to have some skin in the game, if you will. Remember how I talked about Caroline saving her money for summer camp? This is where the skin-in-the-game principle came into play. As they reached middle school age, our girls wanted to attend summer camp, but rather than simply doling out the money, we required each girl to pay a portion of her camp fees. I'm not talking about ten or twenty dollars here; we asked each girl to pay at least two hundred dollars the first year and increased their portion each succeeding year. This was a significant amount of money for a ten-year-old to save, but every year we set a savings goal together, and every year the girls reached that goal by working extra jobs like babysitting and saving any extra money that came their way.

Once the girls were in high school, things changed pretty significantly as we gave them more and more responsibility for their money. We increased their allowance to an amount we thought was fair and required the girls to pay for their clothing and entertainment out of the allowance we gave them. And if they wanted to go to camp, which they did, each girl paid half the fee. They received their allowance every two weeks, same as when we got paid, and if they didn't have enough money for whatever they wanted to buy, they knew they would have to get a job—a lesson in real life.

We also allowed them to have cell phones in high school (I know! So late!), but they were required to pay their portion of the family cell phone bill, anywhere from ten to thirty-five dollars, depending on the type of phone they chose. That really caused each girl to weigh her decision carefully: *Do I really want that smartphone? Because if I got the cheaper, non-smartphone my bill would be smaller.* These are real-life decisions, ones that adults have to make every day, and we were trying to teach our kids how to make adult decisions about money while they still lived under our roof.

Right now you're probably thinking that we were the meanest parents on earth! And at times, our kids probably thought that too. We wanted to make sure that, along with teaching our kids about God and people and life and the Bible, we were also intentionally teaching them how to handle their finances. Each step of their development brought greater and greater financial responsibility.

It wasn't easy all the time. Some of the decisions our kids had to make were very difficult, and I'll be honest, I've wanted to step in and help them out on more than one occasion. But we all struggle with money at times, and Brian and I knew that bailing them out wasn't the best way to help our daughters.

Several years into this process I asked Kate how she felt about how we handled allowances and financial responsibility, and her answer surprised me. She said that at times the lessons were painful, but in the end she was grateful for the training because in college she knew so much more about handling money than most people. She also said she learned that it's very easy to get into trouble with money—that it has to be handled carefully. The two most important lessons she took away were learning to delay gratification (something many adults don't understand) and the value of a budget.

Today, I believe, all three of our daughters are well on their way to freedom in this area because they learned from a very young age the benefit of giving, saving, and spending wisely.

A Word About Mistakes

Maybe you're feeling overwhelmed right now. Maybe you've made some mistakes with money and you need to make some changes. Let me speak a word of grace to you—start small. Make one small change at a time while you commit your finances to God, and I believe he will bless you for it.

> **Start small. Make one small change at a time while you commit your finances to God.**

Maybe the way you have handled money in the past is a heart issue for you. Maybe you have loved material things more than you love God. Do you need to confess this to God and allow him to take first place in your heart? Spend some time identifying the potential idols in your life, especially in the area of finances, and pray for an undivided heart.

Maybe you need to start intentionally teaching your kids about money, but you just don't know how to do it. I've included a list of resources that may help you (see the appendix). And may I encourage you today to, as Nike says, "Just Do It!" Start a three-jar system and talk to your kids especially about the God jar. Open a savings account for your grade-school child and talk about saving for future goals. Give your teenager some financial freedom, but also talk to them about the accountability that comes with it. And always remember the One who has given these gifts to you and your child.

It has been one of our greatest joys to see our daughters grow in the area of their finances. Knowing that they have become young adults who handle their money wisely brings so much comfort to us as parents. And knowing that their hearts want to honor God by stewarding his gifts carefully gives us tremendous hope for their futures.

Consider

1. Why do you think God calls us to steward our money carefully? Is it important to include this in your family's travel plan? Why or why not?

2. Were you given any guidance about handling money when you were younger? If so, what did you learn? What, if anything, do you think you need to change about your spending or saving habits?

3. How do you feel you've done in teaching your kids about money so far? If you feel like you need a boost in this area, check out the resources suggested in the appendix, or check with your church to see if they have recommendations.

PART 4

Our Contribution

By this my Father is glorified, that you bear much
fruit and so prove to be my disciples.
JOHN 15:8

10

STRENGTHENING OUR TIES

Intentional Family Memories

THE SCENE IN OUR HOME PROBABLY LOOKED MUCH LIKE YOURS AT five thirty in the afternoon: hungry kids, tired parents, elevated tempers (mine, usually), and lots of noise. By the time my husband got home from work each night, our house looked like something out of a Steve Martin movie: kids plus chaos equals catastrophe.

This scenario played itself out night after night. Worn-out and frazzled at five o'clock, I'd attempt to make dinner after a busy day of teaching at the college nearby and caring for my kids; the girls would run around the house in a late-afternoon burst of energy; and Brian would walk in the door, tired from his day, wanting nothing more than peace and quiet.

Nobody was happy at five thirty.

Until Buddy Holly came into the picture.

I don't know exactly why it happened, but on one such chaotic day, Brian scooped up the girls and took them upstairs with him when he went to change his clothes, allowing me a few minutes of peace to focus on dinner. Soon I heard music—*Is that our old Buddy Holly CD?*—and squeals of delight—*Is that our daughters?*—coming from our bedroom above me.

Eventually the laughter and singing made me curious, so I crept up the stairs to see what was going on. I peeked into our bedroom to find three little girls jumping on the bed, squealing with laughter, and their dad, now changed into his jeans and a T-shirt, dancing on the floor while all four of them sang "That'll Be the Day" at the top of their lungs.

I'll never forget that scene, and neither will the rest of my family, because Buddy Holly soon became a regular thing for us. During that most difficult time of day when moms tend to yell a little more and dads seem to lose their patience, when everyone is just starving and can't wait one more minute for dinner, we were creating a family memory that has lasted to this day. In fact, Buddy Holly marks a very special time in our family—those carefree years when little girls jumped on the bed and learned every song from one of the first rock and rollers in history.

Even now, every time we hear a Buddy Holly song, we all stop and smile, and of course, we all sing along. We know every word.

Listening to Buddy Holly has bonded us as a family. His music will forever mark us. And it's all because my husband intentionally created a memory with our daughters.

I'm sure you're probably thinking of something similar in your family. Maybe you have inside jokes that you all share. Or maybe you remember a time when you all came together to solve a problem. Or maybe you still laugh about that time in your childhood when your cousin drank too much grape soda and threw up all over the back seat of your grandparents' car.

Memories, good and bad, bind us together as a family. They connect us and strengthen us, and today, perhaps more than ever, strong families matter. But how are strong families built? You and I both know that strong families don't just happen. Families need tending. Parents who intentionally set out to create memories for their kids see the result: a strong family, a bonded family, a family that enjoys one another and enjoys being together.

I'm not talking about a lavish, one-time, Disney World type of memory, although those are fun too. The memories I'm talking about here are those that are seared into our family histories, so much so that they become part of our family DNA.

Take, for instance, half-birthday celebrations. For a child, turning anything-and-a-half is a big deal, so one year I decided to have fun with it. Our local grocery store sells cakes cut in half, so that became the half-birthday cake. I cut a candle in half and placed it in the cake along with the correct number of full-sized ones. And, of course, we got goofy and sang "Happy Half-Birthday to You."

Half-birthdays didn't cost much—just the cost of half a cake and maybe a card—but they sure bonded us. Our girls are grown up and we haven't celebrated half-birthdays for a number of years, but we still remember those celebrations with fondness. We still giggle about the silliness of it all, but we also remember how much that brief celebration mattered to each girl. To this day, September 30 on our online family calendar reads, "Kate's half-birthday. Thou shalt buy cake!" (She especially loves traditions.)

Why Make Family Memories?

Family memories are critical for creating strong family ties. But *why* are they important? I believe that in our overly busy culture, we must choose to either connect or disconnect as a family. Nobody likes that feeling of being disconnected when things get too busy; by creating intentional family memories we can stay just a little more bonded. Our family memories have threefold significance for our children's lives: social, personal, and spiritual.

Social Significance

First, family memories are important because they create lifelong bonds among the members. Our culture is doing everything it can to pull families apart. Sports, school, and even our churches offer a myriad of activities for our kids; organized activities have taken the place of pickup games. Nearly everything in our kids' lives has become scheduled, and as a result, our families are becoming fractured, frazzled, and fragmented.

I think of the Oprah segment I saw years ago during which she interviewed a stay-at-home mom who was completely distraught by the many demands on her time. This poor mother was so busy running kids from activity to activity while trying to tend to her home and volunteer at school that she claimed she didn't have time to go to the bathroom! To me, there's something seriously wrong with that picture.

As parents, it's our job to lead our families in ways that bring us together, not tear us apart. It's not necessarily a bad thing for our kids to be involved in individual activities. But if we find ourselves going in separate directions all the time, every day, we might need to ask ourselves why we choose to invest our time in the activities we do and why we aren't spending time together and bonding as a family.

My friend Cheryce felt the tug of busyness putting strains on her family, so she decided to take action to bring their family closer together through more meaningful memories. She and her husband, Mark, asked their three boys, then ages thirteen, eleven, and eight, if they would be willing to stop playing soccer for one season so that they could spend Saturdays together as a family. To their surprise, the boys readily agreed.

This wasn't just a pulling away from something, though. Cheryce and Mark were intentionally pulling the family together for this season, which they called City Saturdays. Cheryce felt that, even though they lived near Chicago, one of the greatest and most beautiful cities in the world, she and her family didn't know the city as well as they'd like. For six months, they would spend every Saturday in Chicago, exploring a new neighborhood, taking part in a new activity, or visiting a new museum. The draw for the boys? Lunch out in a new restaurant every week!

The plan was set and implemented, and for six months their family bonded over Chicago hot dogs and Chinatown and sailing on Lake Michigan, among many other activities. And no soccer. Cheryce found that not only were their Saturday schedules freed up but much of their week was freed up as well because nobody had to go to soccer practice. Their family could eat dinner together more often, even play games in the evening, and simply enjoy their time together.

David King and Margot Starbuck tackle some myths about the youth sports culture in their book, *Overplayed*. They say that over twenty-one million kids between the ages of six and seventeen are now enrolled in youth sports each year.[1] Yes, that's a huge number of kids, but this tells me two things: First, parents feel extreme pressure to put their kids in sports, even when the kids are very young. Second (and here's the good news), nobody will miss your child if he or she opts out.

The authors ask parents to think counterculturally when it comes to youth sports:

> Without ever asking why, we are subjecting our kids to systems that we don't fully understand and ones that may actually harm them. In the beginning we might register our children for sports with no higher expectations than that they'll get a little exercise and have fun with friends. Then we might bump them up a league to help them get the kind of "skill development" that will help them succeed against more competitive players. Before we know it, we can't remember the last weekend our family spent in the same city or one that cost us less than $400. We find ourselves stretched physically, financially, and emotionally. And we wonder how we ended up like this.[2]

And it's not just sports—so many other activities can pull our families apart as well. Have you asked your kids what *they* want to do? Have you asked them if they really want to play sports? Have you thought through *why* you have enrolled your child in music or theater or kickboxing? Driven by today's American culture, parents often believe that if their kids don't play sports or aren't involved in some other activity outside the home, then their lives won't be successful. But that argument plays on parents' fears and emotions. We can't fear being a little countercultural when it comes to protecting time together as a family, because that time together makes us stronger.

> **We can't fear being a little countercultural when it comes to protecting time together as a family.**

We like to say that our daughter Kate was given a height advantage. She is very close to six feet two inches tall today, and even as a young girl, she was tall for her age. So obviously, basketball. Her basketball-playing dad was thrilled when she was allowed to join the boys' team in our local youth league. He was also thrilled when she was asked to attend several summer basketball clinics, even more so when she joined a traveling basketball team in junior high.

As Kate's basketball playing took more and more of her time, we found our family spending less and less time together. The more Kate played basketball, however, the less she enjoyed it. She felt extreme pressure to perform for her coaches, but the pressure diminished her ability to play well. She loved the accolades from her dad, but deep inside she wasn't loving time on the court.

Finally, as the time for basketball tryouts approached during Kate's sophomore year in high school, she bravely sat us down and told us that she didn't want to play basketball anymore. Now, I'm not an athlete—I've never even played one on TV—so this announcement didn't shock, startle, or sadden me one bit. I was secretly happy to move on from this sport that took so much of our family's time and attention.

But Brian had to work through some things. Was he reliving his glory days through his daughter? Was he demanding too much of her? Was their relationship based solely on basketball? If he were perfectly honest, he'd say that he did experience a brief moment of disappointment. But he had seen our daughter feeling the pressure on the court, he knew she was capable of so much more than basketball, and he knew that this was the right decision for her.

Once Kate's decision was made (and it *was* her decision, not ours), things in our home changed. We were able to focus on our relationships with one another again. Kate seemed happier. And she was able to pursue other interests that she would not have had time for earlier. For us and especially for her, Kate's decision to stop playing basketball was a good one.

Lest you think I'm opposed to sports, let me just say that's not the case at all. If your child loves the sport she plays and you can figure out how the sport fits into your family (and not the other way around), I say go for it. We want our children to flourish and to use the gifts God has given them. Several of my closest friends have children who have played collegiate sports, and their families have survived, even thrived, during these busy seasons. I do think, however, that we must ask our kids what feels right for them rather than pushing them to do too much too soon.

Here's the thing: sports, clubs, musical groups . . . all these things can be very good in and of themselves, but taken to an extreme, they can pull our families apart. We must be willing to be countercultural and say no when these activities threaten our families or our kids. As King and Starbuck say, "If our commitments to our faith communities and neighbors and those in need have been marginalized by athletic commitments, it may be time to reexamine the way we're using our time."[3]

Personal Significance

I've already mentioned that I grew up on an Illinois grain farm; that place formed much of who I became as an adult. But more than that, it was the people around me who made a difference in my life. My grandparents, aunt, uncle, and cousins lived so close that I could walk or ride my bike to their houses any time I wanted. We shared holidays and birthdays together. I knew that no matter what, these people were with me and *for* me—they were my people and, in many ways, they still are.

Children first begin to sense who they are in the family—it's a training ground for personal growth. When we, as parents, intentionally foster a home of loving acceptance, we are laying a foundation that will last our children's lifetime. Part of discipling our kids is creating an atmosphere that will encourage their growth as individuals. Happy family memories will help our kids flourish later in life.

I know, however, that not everyone has warm memories of childhood. Some people grew up in very difficult situations, and if so, my heart grieves with you. If you suffered through a difficult childhood, know this: Christ came to wipe your tears away and to make *all* things new, including your past. In him we can start a new life. Jesus is in the restoration business, and he wants to restore you and your family. In him our past can be transformed, in him our relationships can be made new, and in him we can find flourishing. If you want to see a change in your home, why not start by creating some positive memories for your children today? Even small, seemingly insignificant moments can turn into special memories.

One of Kate's and Caroline's earliest memories took place in the pink-tiled bathroom in our small house on President Street. Each morning, as Brian got ready for work, the girls would squeeze into the tiny bathroom and huddle on the edge of the tub to watch him shave. They would talk about the upcoming day, but mostly they would sing.

Daddy led: "What can wash away my sins?"

And the girls followed: "Nothing but the blood of Jesus!"

"What can make me whole again?"

"Nothing but the blood of Jesus!"[4]

As soon as they'd hear the shower turn off, they'd scamper to the bathroom door and wait until Daddy let them in. Wherever I was in the house, I could hear them singing at the top of their lungs. Every morning it was the same thing. Singing this song with the girls seemed a simple moment, perhaps even an insignificant one. But each girl points to that memory today as one that matters greatly to her. And I believe that in their lonely moments, my girls look back on their growing-up years and remember that they belong, not just in that tiny pink bathroom huddled on the side of the tub, not just in our house on President Street, not just in our little "Party of Five," but also, most significantly, to Jesus.

This is what family memories do for us. They connect us. They remind us that we are not just individuals, but we are members of a unit—a family—and when one member laughs, we all laugh; when one hurts, we all hurt. Memories teach our kids that they belong, that they are a part of something bigger than themselves, and that no matter where they are in the world, they are loved.

Spiritual Significance

The Bible is full of memories. In the Old Testament narrative God often tells his people to remember certain events, to look back, so that they will be able to tell their children about his faithfulness. When we create family memories, we remind our children that God is still at work in our families, that he has been faithful to us in the past and will be faithful to us in the future.

In Joshua 3 and 4, we find the Israelites on the brink of the most important move of their lives. God has already done amazing things for his people—he has rescued them from slavery in Egypt by helping them cross the Red Sea, he has provided manna and quail for them as they wandered in the desert for forty years, and he has given them rules that will help them live healthy, holy lives.

At this point in the narrative, we find the twelve tribes of Israel ready, after all those years of wandering, to cross into the land that God is giving them. There they stand on the edge of the Jordan River—men, women, children, flocks, herds, and possessions—eager to take possession of the land that is rightfully theirs. But how will they get across? The river is too wide, too fast, and too dangerous, and there are no bridges.

Once again God intervenes. He tells the priests who are carrying the ark of the covenant to step into the water with the ark on their shoulders. The minute their feet touch the water, the water moves away, parting before them just like the Red Sea did all those years earlier, which, obviously, the Israelites remember.

> So when the people set out from their tents to pass over the Jordan with the priests bearing the ark of the covenant before the people, and as soon as those bearing the ark had come as far as the Jordan, and the feet of the priests bearing the ark were dipped in the brink of the water (now the Jordan overflows all its banks throughout the time of harvest), the waters coming down from above stood and rose up in a heap very far away. . . . Now the priests bearing the ark of the covenant of the LORD stood firmly on dry ground in the midst of the Jordan, and all Israel was passing over on dry ground until all the nation finished passing over the Jordan. (Josh. 3:14–17)

It certainly must have been quite a sight, and I'd guess that it took a while for everyone to get across. Yet the Lord never left them, and the waters never crashed down until every person had safely crossed through the river. Before God moved the water back in place, after the last priest stepped safely to the other side, he told Joshua to do something significant to mark the occasion.

The leaders of the twelve tribes were each to take a large rock from the middle of the Jordan River and place it on the riverbank to commemorate what God had done. These stones, God said, were to remain there forever as a marker, a remembrance of God's protection over his people.

> And those twelve stones, which they took out of the Jordan, Joshua set up at Gilgal. And he said to the people of Israel, "When your children ask their fathers in times to come, 'What do these stones mean?' then you shall let your children know, 'Israel passed over this Jordan on dry ground.' For the LORD your God dried up the waters of the Jordan for you until you passed over, as the LORD your God did to the Red Sea, which he dried up for us until we passed over, so that all the peoples of the earth may know that the hand of the LORD is mighty, that you may fear the LORD your God forever." (Josh. 4:20–24)

I love how God is so intentional about teaching the children. The phrases, "When your children ask their fathers" and "You shall let your children know" tell us that God wants us to remember what he's done for us and to teach our children about his faithfulness.

Our own family has a few "stones of remembrance," and perhaps you do too. These markers remind us of God's faithfulness to us in certain places. And they help our children see that our families are created by God for his purposes.

God miraculously saved Caroline's life in a park in the middle of Lake Geneva, Wisconsin, when she was four years old. Our family had been attending a church camp there, and one night everyone (minus Brian and a newborn Julia) took a walk into town for ice cream.

What started as a fun-filled, joyful time very quickly became a frightening event when a sudden thunderstorm quickly turned into a tornado. We ran for cover, but the shelter was too far for me to carry Caroline, so someone in our group placed her and another little girl into a wagon and ran like crazy. Seriously, when I think of chaos, I think of that moment. The sky turned black; the lake churned right beside us; the bells on top of the sailboats clanged like mad; and everywhere, people screamed and ran for their lives.

I yelled above the noise to tell six-year-old Kate to run as fast as her legs would take her while trying to keep an eye on Caroline in the wagon behind me. Once Kate reached the shelter, I turned around to check on Caroline's progress just as the wagon rolled past a huge, old maple tree—one that had probably been in that park for a hundred years. A woman from our church was standing near the tree directing people to the shelter, and just as I turned around, I saw her eyes grow huge as she yelled, "Move! Move! Move!"

And then . . . one . . . two . . . three . . . seconds after my precious four-year-old daughter rolled past it, that tree came crashing down to the earth, completely uprooted.

The next day the town was without water and electricity, so everyone at camp packed up and headed home, but on our way out of town we stopped at the park to look at that uprooted tree. It was every bit as big as I remembered; it would have easily killed anyone who got caught underneath its weight. I took a picture of the uprooted tree so that we could all remember God's faithfulness to us and his loving protection over Caroline.

I know that God spared my daughter's life that day. I know it like I know the smell of my babies' skin. And to this day, that photo of a fallen tree in a park in Lake Geneva serves to remind us of the way God protected Caroline. It is a stone of remembrance in our family.

God's faithfulness is evident all around us every day.

God's faithfulness is evident all around us every day, and his protection is real. Stones of remembrance help us keep track of the ways God has been faithful to us or protected us. They bind us to one another, making our families stronger. So be on the lookout and share them with your children, just like the Israelites did.

Do You Create Family Memories?

You've probably thought of some of your own family memories as you've been reading this chapter. You've probably thought, *Yeah, our family does silly things too. We sing goofy songs. We've got rituals just like you do.* That's awesome! I'm so glad there are crazy families out there who may be just as weird and goofy as we are.

But let me ask you something: What are you doing within your unique family to create an atmosphere of togetherness? Are you spending time together over meals, retelling stories of fun times you've shared together over the years, or are you quickly grabbing food as you shuttle your kids to rehearsal or practice? Are you taking time to cultivate family memories, or are you too busy to create new ones?

One of the best ways to retain and strengthen bonds within a family, research tells us, is by sharing regular meals together. In fact, having family meals is one of the main predictors that your children will succeed. One author wrote, "A recent wave of research shows that children who eat dinner with their families are less likely to drink, smoke, do drugs, get pregnant, commit suicide, and develop eating disorders. Additional research found that children who enjoy family meals have larger vocabularies, better manners, healthier diets, and higher self-esteem."[5] These seem like lofty claims, I know, but studies show they are true.

Further, researchers have found that children who know their family history—things such as where their grandparents grew up and how their parents met—have a stronger sense of control over their lives. This "Do You Know?" scale has become one of the best indicators of a child's emotional health and personal satisfaction. Turns out that our family narrative—those stories we tell over and over again—is actually helpful for increasing our child's self-confidence.[6]

And where are those stories most often told? At the dinner table.

We all have busy seasons; I completely understand that. But if running around frantically from one thing to another has become the norm in your family, you might need to step back and ask why.

Why are we choosing busy over bonding?

Why are we rushing instead of relaxing?

Why are we valuing individuality over family togetherness?

Why are we spending money we might not have on activities our kids might not even want to participate in?

You may have your own why question to ask here. Start today by asking your kids, "Why do you like being in _____?" Have a discussion. Look at Scripture. Pray.

And find your sweet spot as a family. Together.

Consider

1. Why do you think creating family memories is important? Is it important to include this in your family's travel plan? Why or why not?
2. What are some of your favorite family memories? Why do you think these memories have made an impact on your family?
3. Do you ever find yourself wishing your child would drop an activity? Which one(s)? Why?
4. How many times a week does your family sit down to eat a meal together? Is there anything you feel you could or should change so that you can come together more often?
5. Spend some time this week talking to your kids about God's faithfulness to your family. Share a couple memories (or perhaps create your own stones of remembrance) and thank God for his goodness to you.

11

SAME BUT DIFFERENT

Intentional Cultural Awareness

A SIMPLE CHEDDAR CHEESE SANDWICH ON WHITE BREAD, PUR-chased from a cart on the street near our hotel—this was my first meal in England circa 1984. Simple yet wholesome, and perfect for a hungry college student just off her first international flight.

There was something so familiar about that sandwich—just cheese and bread. I knew those components, yet the combination tasted so different from any cheese sandwich I had ever eaten. The cheddar, for starters, wasn't the orange color I was familiar with; instead, it was white—and flavorful. And the bread wasn't the squishy, stick-to-the-top-of-your-mouth kind that I grew up with. Instead, its texture was firm and slightly crumbly, which I now know is because the flour they use is less processed than our American version. Familiar, yet unfamiliar.

Same but different.

I encountered similarities and differences around every corner during my summer studying in England. Tea? Yes, but more full-bodied than the tea I drank at home. And served with cream and sugar. Cars? Of course, but smaller. And the people drove on the other side of the road. Music? Yes, but with a different tone and a different beat.

And the language? Oh, it's technically the same, but so many of the words sound different to my ears and have entirely different meanings. And as I traveled north, the words began to sound almost foreign.

Same but different.

From the moment we landed and began exploring the city of London, I felt as if I had found my second home. Well over thirty years later, I still love England. It has transformed me in significant ways.

On that trip, my eyes were opened to the similarities and differences between Americans and the British, and my worldview was forever changed. I remember the exact moment my worldview shifted. I was riding the tube—London's version of the New York subway or the Chicago "L"—just observing the people around me. I knew that, aside from my study-abroad friends and myself, everyone on the train was a Londoner; I could tell by their fair skin (remember, it was the early eighties) and their accents (of course), but mostly by the looks on their faces.

One man, standing in the center aisle of the train car, particularly caught my eye—a businessman in a dark suit and rumpled trench coat. With a briefcase in one hand and a newspaper folded up under his arm, he grasped the gray plastic ring above his head with his free hand. His face reflected utter gloom.

I watched this man for a while as we rode the train together; I don't think he noticed me. His eyes barely took in the scene around him, perhaps because he had done this commute a thousand times before, or perhaps because he had worries on his mind, or perhaps just because he had had a hard day. But the look of deep sadness never left him.

I'd have thought it was just him, but I had noticed the same look in others' eyes everywhere I went in the few weeks I had been in the country—from the waitress who served me tea and scones to the girl standing behind the shop counter to the mums pushing their babies in their prams. Was it a longing? A lack of purpose? Or a lack of hope?

On the tube that day, I realized something that might have been a no-brainer to someone else but became significant to me: these people were different from me in many ways, yet the same. We all needed rest from the world. We all needed rescuing. We all needed a Savior.

Same but different.

This sudden awareness caught me by surprise and changed me forever.

I had been raised in the church. I had visited big cities. I had naively thought that, because we shared a language, the British people would be much like my Midwestern American friends who valued faith. What I quickly realized was that the Christianity of England was very different from the Christianity I had grown up in; faith in God was not highly valued the way I had seen it valued at home. Already Christianity in England was in decline (it would take several decades before we would experience a similar reality in the United States), and I could see the hopelessness on people's faces everywhere I went.

Of course there were folks in England with deep, abiding faith in Christ back in the early eighties, just as there are today. But since that time, the number of people who describe themselves as Anglican, a member of the established Church of England, has been cut in half. Today the people who describe themselves as having no religion outnumber those who consider themselves Christians, which includes "Anglicans, Catholics and other denominations."[1] Religious decline in the United Kingdom shows no sign of slowing down.

This decline in religious interest was taking place in America as well, but as a young, naive college student, I didn't know that. It took traveling to another country—one similar in many ways, yet vastly different—to open my eyes to the deep spiritual needs of the world.

What Is Cultural Awareness?

Cultural awareness, sometimes called "cultural sensitivity" or "cultural empathy," is recognizing that "cultural differences and similarities between people exist without assigning them a value—positive or negative, better or worse, right or wrong. It simply means that you are aware that people are not all the same and that you recognize that your culture is no better than any other culture."[2]

Seems simple enough, right? But until we truly engage people of other cultures and try to understand them, we often aren't aware of our personal biases. Discovering them can make us feel less than intelligent, awkward, confused, or embarrassed. And that never feels good. The work of getting to really know someone is not simple; often it's difficult and messy. We have to admit our personal biases and put them aside.

In her wonderful novel, *To Kill a Mockingbird*, Harper Lee gives us a picture of what it means to become aware of people who are different from us. Atticus Finch, a lawyer, a leader in his community, and a man of deep integrity and wisdom, is father to Scout and Jem, two young children growing up in the segregated South of the 1930s. The two children learn one summer what it means to be different, both racially and economically.

> **Until we truly engage people of other cultures . . . we often aren't aware of our personal biases.**

One day, a young boy named Walter Cunningham joins the family for lunch. His manners are crude, and his appetite for syrup is huge, but he knows how to talk sharecropping with Atticus just like a grown up. Walter is a mystery to Scout in many ways, so when she calls him out on his table manners, she doesn't understand why she finds herself in trouble with the family's African American maid.

Later, Atticus explains an important life lesson to his young daughter. "If you can learn a simple trick, Scout, you'll get along a lot better with all kinds of folks. You never really understand a person until you consider things from his point of view . . . until you climb into his skin and walk around in it."[3] In other words, we've got to learn to see things from the perspective of others, and sometimes that's hard work.

Mom and Dad, please hear this: intentionally helping our kids become culturally aware can feel a little uncomfortable, and it may feel a bit scary at times, but the work it takes will be worth it. Cultural awareness opens our kids to new experiences and new people, and it just might lead them to discover a new passion or purpose for their future.

Cultural Awareness in the Bible

There's a passage of Scripture that illustrates the idea of "same but different," or actually "different but same," perfectly. In Acts 10 we read about Cornelius, a Roman officer who was a devout follower of God. During his prayer time one day, Cornelius had a vision of an angel of God who told him to seek out Peter.

Peter also had a vision during his prayer time, but his vision was a little different. Three times, Peter saw a large sheet filled with all kinds of animals, reptiles, and birds, and three times God told him it was OK to eat any of these animals (Acts 10:11–16). Peter, being a devout Jew, protested a bit, but after the third time, he knew something was up. He was confused, but just then, Cornelius's men knocked on his door.

What we see in Acts 10 is a beautiful picture of God opening up the eyes of both of these men to their cultural similarities and differences for a very special purpose.

Their differences could not have been more stark. As a Roman, Cornelius was obviously a Gentile and not schooled in Jewish laws and customs. Peter was a devout Jew, so much so that he only ate kosher food and primarily associated with other Jews. As Peter remarks in verse 28, it was against Jewish laws to enter the home of a Gentile.

But there was one important similarity between these men: they both recognized their need for a Savior. Peter had already experienced that salvation. He had known Jesus personally, traveled with him, and witnessed his death and resurrection. Peter was sure that Jesus was the Christ, but he had not yet come to realize that the message of Christ was for all people, not just Jews. Cornelius, on the other hand, had a sense of his need for salvation, but he did not know how to obtain it.

In his divine providence, God brought the two men together to teach them something critical about salvation: that it is for *everyone* who believes. In Acts 10:34–35 we read, "So Peter opened his mouth and said: 'Truly I understand that God shows no partiality, but in every nation anyone who fears him and does what is right is acceptable to him.'" Later, the apostle Paul would write, "For by grace you have been saved through faith. And this is not your own doing; it is the gift of God" (Eph. 2:8). Peter and Cornelius both learned an important lesson about God's gift of grace that day, and they did it by opening their hearts to the Holy Spirit's leading and by taking steps to begin to understand the customs of another culture.

How Can I Instill Cultural Awareness in My Kids?

We as parents have to become convinced that cultural awareness is important and make it a priority to expose our kids to different cultures. We've got to realize that because of political upheaval and advances in technology and transportation, people are moving around the world more than ever before, and our children will most likely encounter people from other countries and cultures much more often than we did. We can begin to instill cultural awareness by simply having conversations with our kids about current events, reading books about other cultures, or watching movies set in other countries. But that's just a start.

It's important to get out of our comfort zones and visit places that are different from where we live to expose our kids to different cultures. My friend Cheryce did that with her family on City Saturdays when they visited Chinatown and other ethnic neighborhoods in Chicago. We can visit an art museum and talk to our kids about various styles of art and the cultures from which they came. Or we can serve in a ministry based in another culture.

When Kate and Caroline were in high school, they tutored every week in Chicago's Austin neighborhood at an after-school program called By the Hand Club for Kids. The students they served grew up in some of the city's most violent and poverty-stricken neighborhoods, and, because of those obstacles, they were struggling in school. As the weeks and months went by, my girls learned about the way these kids lived, the difficulties they encountered just to get to school every day, and how poverty inhibits learning. This program focuses on education, of course, but by also meeting basic needs, such as a healthy dinner, safe passage to and from the program, and exposure to the gospel, the children begin to excel in school and to have a vision for a future that includes college and a life of hope. My girls learned an important lesson through that experience— that everyone deserves safety, an education, and especially, hope.

While I believe that encouraging experiences such as these are a start in exposing our children to other cultures, the best way I know to help increase cultural awareness in our kids is to travel. I subscribe to this famous adage: "The world is a book and those who do not travel read only one page."

Why Travel?

Travel is one of my greatest passions in life—just ask my kids! It's probably in my DNA. My grandfather Earl, also a globe-trotter, regularly dragged my grandmother, whom he affectionately called "Toots," away from the sofa, where she enjoyed crossword puzzles and soap operas, to places I had never heard of. Toots and Earl spent years exploring the world—from Hawaii to Hong Kong to Helsinki. Each time they returned home, I'd listen to their stories for hours and look at their photos with keen interest, each one sparking my imagination about the world beyond our cornfields.

Over the years our family has traveled with a purpose. Oh yes, we've traveled for fun too, but sometimes we've traveled to intentionally develop cultural awareness in our kids. We've served on mission trips together, and one time when our girls were very young, we visited missionary friends in Brazil. Is this type of travel a sacrifice of both time and money? Yes, for sure. But is it worth it? Yes. Here are just five of the reasons I believe travel is valuable.

First, travel exposes us to other people. Just as I learned as a college student in England, when I travel, I realize again that not everyone lives the way I do, believes what I do, or experiences life as I do. We're all different, but we all need the same basic things: food, shelter, love, hope. As I mentioned earlier, our kids will one day be working in an environment where they will encounter people who are unlike them. Travel is one way to begin to prepare our kids to interact well with all types of people.

Second, travel exposes our weaknesses. Travel can be stressful at times. It can be tiring. We may get lost or frustrated with one another. And sometimes someone in the family runs low on blood sugar and sits down on a curb, refusing to take one more step (not that we've had any experience with that or anything). We're human, and travel reminds us that we need grace and forgiveness in equal measure.

Third, travel teaches us important life skills. Much to my dismay, my kids have learned to get around with the assistance of Google Maps and GPS, but there are times when I force them to use a real live map, because map reading is an important life skill. Also, when we travel, I often make my kids responsible for planning part of the trip—another important skill.

Sometimes we need to ask for help from others, possibly even someone who doesn't speak our language. Learning to communicate is yet another critical life skill. In the end, getting from point A to point B can feel like an important accomplishment to our kids, and that sense of pride in acquiring these skills may help them realize they can do other things too!

Fourth, travel shows us the majesty of God. History, art, architecture, and especially nature can all play a part in revealing God's awesome attributes to our kids. There's nothing like seeing the sunrise over the eastern edge of the Grand Canyon or standing next to the powerful pounding of the ocean to cause us to revel in the glory of God. Everywhere I look, every time I travel, I see God's great, creative hand in nature, and I want my kids to see and appreciate that too.

Finally, travel shows us the world's need. Every time I travel—*every time*—I come face-to-face with poverty, both financial and spiritual. And every time, I am reminded that the only solution to the poverty of this world is the Savior who loves them. Even in the wealthiest of countries there is financial and spiritual bankruptcy. When I travel with my kids, I pray that they catch a glimpse of the true needs of the world too.

Awareness Shows Us the Compassion of God

As we interact with people from other cultures, we begin to understand the compassion of God. God is the creator of all people of all cultures and, as 2 Peter 3:9 tells us, he does not want any to perish. None. Each one of his children is precious to him, and we begin to get a small glimpse of this when we get to know people who are different from us yet somehow the same.

I grew up in a small farming community. I went to school with the same people until I went to college. Most of the kids I grew up with looked pretty much like me, and although not everyone lived on a farm, we all shared a common culture. Let's just say that my educational experience wasn't very diverse.

Here's the thing: where I grew up and the way I grew up wasn't *wrong*. In fact, the community where I was raised is filled with some of the most loving, caring, compassionate people I've ever met. But I needed to seek out opportunities to get to know people who weren't just like me.

My children, unlike me, went to the elementary school just around the corner from our home, which we intentionally chose because of its diverse student body. Their classes were made up of children of various ethnic backgrounds, largely because the apartment complex down the street housed refugees from other countries. In any given year, our daughters had friends from as far away as Bosnia, Somalia, or Myanmar, and they learned that, although we may eat different foods and wear different clothes, all children like to laugh, tease, and play games on the playground. And I've never met a child who doesn't like chocolate chip cookies!

The good news is that Christ died for the sins of the *whole* world—people of every culture, every tongue, every tribe, and every nation!

Interacting with children from other cultures was a wonderful but challenging part of their education, and it taught our daughters many important life lessons. We still marvel at one girl who entered my daughter's second grade class one November Monday, having just arrived over the weekend from her war-torn country. She knew not a word of English, and she was quiet and scared. But by the end of the year, she was fluent in English, had many friends, and had surpassed most of her classmates in math. I have often pointed to her example of determination and success to inspire my children to work hard, no matter what their obstacles may be.

But here's the most important lesson I hope my girls took away from their culturally diverse schools: the good news is that Christ died for the sins of the *whole* world—people of every culture, every tongue, every tribe, and every nation! We may be different in many ways from our classmates or the people down the street from us, but we all have a common need: to have our sins removed, to be redeemed by God, to be changed by the work that Jesus came to do.

I want my children to hold on to that gospel vision, to believe that the sacrifice that has bought their salvation wasn't just for them but for everyone. As C. Herbert Woolston's classic Sunday school song says, "Jesus loves the little children, all the children of the world." This is the vision I wanted my children to catch. And I want them to take that with them wherever they go.

What if an intentional awareness of other cultures sparked a passion for missions in your child? What if he or she became interested in sharing the gospel in a large city? What if our kids took the Great Commission (Matt. 28:19–20) seriously and began making disciples themselves? Could an increased awareness of the needs of the world spark a new passion in your child?

Someday your children will leave your nest (trust me, it does happen), and they will have a myriad of choices ahead of them about where they will live, whether they will continue their education, and what type of career they might pursue. No matter what they do or where they go, I want my kids to remember that we are here to shine the light of Jesus into every corner of this dark world.

Consider

1. Why do you think cultural awareness is important? Is it important to include this in your family's travel plan? Why or why not?
2. What is one way your kids have been exposed to a culture different from their own?
3. Think of your ancestry and where your parents or grandparents have come from. What are some of the ways your culture today is the same as that of your ancestors, and what are some ways it is different?
4. If you could show your children one place in the world or give them one experience, where or what would it be? Why? Start to pray and dream today about where you might take your kids and how God might use that experience in the lives of your children and in your family.

12

THE LONG WALK TOWARD TRUST

Intentionally Letting Go

ON THE MORNING OF SEPTEMBER 11, 2001, I MADE COFFEE, DRESSED my children for school, and got ready for the day. I was thinking about the errands I would run that day, who needed new jeans before cold weather set in, and what we'd have for dinner that night. I was *not* thinking about the safety or security of my kids.

Until the phone rang and my husband said, "Turn on the news." And suddenly our world came crashing down.

I remember every detail of that day. Crumpling to the floor in tears and fear. Gathering my girls around to pray. Trying, feebly, to explain this evil act to three little girls who had never known a day of terror in their lives.

Someone from the school called to say that the day was going to proceed as usual to give kids as much a sense of normalcy as possible. The mental wrangling it took just to walk them to the door of the school and hand them over to their teachers for the day was grueling. Never before had I wondered if my children would be safe at school.

Never again would I *not* wonder.

September 11, 2001, I believe, changed the way we view history, politics, and the trajectory of our country. That day also changed the way we parent our children.

Parents, this chapter is for your own discipleship. While these thoughts do ultimately affect your children, I am writing with you in mind because

I believe this is one of the hardest yet most important aspects of being a parent: letting go.

Who's in Control?

After 9/11, I noticed a shift among parents toward wanting greater control over their children. Perhaps our lives felt too out of control after 9/11, or perhaps the trend was already starting. In any case, many parents began to seek a sense of security by controlling their children's activities more than in the past.

In the early 1990s, long before 9/11, a new term was coined for behavior that we now all readily recognize. The term may make you squirm or it may make you laugh; some may even proudly claim it for themselves. Nevertheless, this term has become part of our vernacular—we all know what it means: *helicopter parents*.

Several years ago, as helicopter parenting was just beginning to get a lot of media attention, I asked my college writing class to read and respond to an article about this phenomenon. As we discussed the reading, I asked my students, "Can any of you relate to this?" thinking that, of course, none of *my* students would have helicopter parents. About half the class raised their hands. One young man even said, "My mom calls me at least five times a day."

I still haven't gotten over that one.

In recent years the problem has only increased. Parents have actually called me regarding their college student's progress in class. (One tip: don't *ever* call your child's professor unless it is an extreme family emergency.) Research now indicates that my experience isn't unusual, and stories abound of students who cannot advocate for themselves with their professors because they are so used to having their parents do it for them.[1]

My husband has also reported examples of helicopter parenting. One parent wanted to "interview" him to determine whether the company where he works would be a good fit for their child. (Trust me, it wasn't.) Other friends have reported parents asking to sit in on their child's interview or negotiate their child's salary.

We all have stories, I'm sure, of parenting gone off the rails. Today we've even softened the term from *helicopter parenting* to *over-parenting*. Others call it *intensive parenting,*[2] or even *lawnmower parenting,*[3] a term that means smoothing over or mowing down the rough spots in our children's lives. Whatever you choose to call it, it's too much.

What is it that these excessively vigilant parents (and if I'm honest I have to include myself in this category from time to time) have in common? Control. We like to have it, we like to exhibit it, and we like to feel as if we have some semblance of it, even when we really don't. We use cell phones to stay in constant contact with our children, even monitor their whereabouts using GPS technology. We carefully structure our children's play dates and become overly involved in their education.

This behavior doesn't just fuel our anxiety and frustrate other adults. It negatively affects our children. Take, for example, the story of a Montessori school that was forced to cancel a field trip because too many parents signed up to chaperone. Why was this a problem? The school couldn't accommodate that many adults, but not one parent was willing to step out of the field trip so that their child could actually attend.[4] Or another sad example of the child who told a researcher, "I wish my parents had some hobby other than me."[5]

In this age of helicopter, lawnmower, intense parenting, we have made this job of raising our children, which is really a calling and a gift from God, all about us. Of course we love our children, and we probably begin to over-parent *because* we love our children so intensely, but somewhere along the line our connection to our children becomes something we possess, an obsession for some, that we cannot give up.

Trust me, I have been that parent. Just ask my husband who stood next to me, laughing, when I asked a teacher during a prekindergarten open house how she could help my child who was already reading. Would my daughter have enough opportunities for growth and challenge? Did the school offer a gifted program for kindergarteners? The wise teacher simply smiled and graciously answered my questions, but I knew I had overstepped my boundaries and let my fears for my child spill into uncharted territory.

That's why I feel more strongly about this chapter than perhaps any other in this book. Because I can be that parent who wants so much to control my child's schooling, friendships, relationship with God, and . . . well, everything! And I can leave God's sovereign work—his complete authority and control over their lives—completely out of the picture.

What happens when I forget that God is sovereign over my children? I begin to play God, or at least try to, thinking I know what's best for my child, when really, *he* is what's best for them. His plan, not mine, is best. I want to hunker down with my kids, create a bubble around them to keep them safe. But safety is a false hope and an idol.

His plan, not mine, is best.

Almost twenty years ago, dear friends left our community to plant a church in Chicago. This was a time when there were very few Bible-teaching churches there, and our friends felt a very clear call from God to leave the comfort of the suburbs for life in the city. Someone asked about their kids, who were very young then, and I will never forget our friend's response: "The safest place for my children is in the center of God's will. My children aren't any safer in the suburbs if they are outside of God's will."

So when my daughter wants to follow God's clear call on her life to a city eight hundred miles away, I pray hard and trust God's plan. And when another daughter feels God directing her to a city on the opposite coast, two thousand miles away, I pray some more and trust that God has her in his care. My own faith grows when I choose to trust God's sovereign plan over my children.

Parents, for the sake of our children and for the sake of our own spiritual lives, we must begin the process of letting go right now. Today. No matter how old our children are.

What Do I Mean by *Letting Go*?

Let me define what I mean by *letting go*. First, I'm talking about figuratively letting go, letting go in the heart. I mean willfully releasing our children to grow and mature in faith for their good and also for the good of the world. Our children will bless the world around them if they courageously step out, use their gifts, and share their faith. We must allow them, even encourage them, to do this.

I'm also talking about literally letting go. Finding the courage to step out into the world won't just happen for our kids. It takes years of intentional training and encouraging our kids to take small steps toward independence, confidence, and responsibility. These steps toward adulthood will naturally be steps away from our nurture and care. As difficult as it is to consider, these steps are good and right and necessary.

I think of the letting-go process like teaching a child to ride a two-wheel bicycle. At first we hold on loosely as they wobble and try to figure it out, but then we let go altogether and watch them take off. Sometimes they fall, but we're there to help them get back on that bike until they can ride by themselves.

The funny thing is, we laugh and cheer and enjoy every moment of teaching our kids to ride a bike. We're excited that they have finally mastered a new skill, one that will give them increased freedom and independence. So why don't we do that when we take them to college, or help them move into their first apartment, or guide them in decisions that will help launch them toward adulthood?

Could it be that somewhere along the parenting journey, we have forgotten to let go?

Some of you, I realize, will not see things in the same light. You will read Scripture and interpret the parents' role as something much different than I do. That's OK. I believe we want the same thing: to glorify God through our families. Please hear, though, that the deeper issue is not whether our children live under our roofs until marriage, whether or not they go to college, or whether they live next door or on the other side of the country. The real issue is whether we can release control and allow the sovereign God to rule in the lives of our kids.

Learning from Personal Experience

Listen, I understand that the world is a scary place right now and that parenting, as I've often heard from wise friends a few years ahead of me in this parenting journey, is not for the faint of heart. Over the years, I've fielded many hypothetical questions like the following from fearful parents (and I may have asked a few myself):

Why should I let go when it hurts so much?
Why should I let go when the world is so big and crazy and dangerous?
Why should I let go when my kids are so young?
Don't I know what's best for my child?

I understand your concerns. I really do. I had them myself as we raised three daughters in a world that seems more insane every single day. I have, at times, wanted to keep them near, huddle them close, and never, ever let them go. I felt keenly afraid on 9/11 and desperately hoped I could keep my children safe by keeping them close.

But my life experience has taught me something else. I learned at an early age that no matter how much I love my children, no matter what I do to provide a loving home or a carefully structured environment, ultimately, I cannot keep them safe. My children are safest in God's hands, and that is why I must continually remember to let go.

In the summer of 1974, I was a carefree eleven-year-old who rode her bicycle down country lanes, wandered through Illinois cornfields, and loved her family dearly. I was an imaginative child who drank in books like water, made up glamorous lives for her Barbies, and played cowboys and Indians in the back yard with her brother.

One week that August, my only brother, Chris, who was nine years old, went to summer camp and never came home. He drowned in a strange and mysterious accident that week, one that I've never completely understood and won't know all the answers to until I meet him again one day in eternity. As difficult as that experience was, and although my brother died, I believe God was and still is sovereign over his life.

Eighteen years later, I lay in a hospital bed holding my firstborn child, and in that moment I felt the weight of grief over losing my brother yet again, because I knew that my daughter, whom I already loved with my entire heart, could be taken from me just as quickly. I knew the fragility of life. I knew that I could not keep her safe, even though I wanted to. But I also knew that she was ultimately a gift from God and that he deserved my complete trust in his sovereign care over her.

In those first few moments, I held my daughter in my arms and said what must have sounded like crazy talk to my husband: "I feel like my job from here on out is to help her not need me anymore." As strange as those words were, they were my way of beginning the process of letting go, of loosening my grip, of telling God that I would trust him with my child. These words were my first feeble attempts to answer my own why questions.

A Biblical Model of Letting Go

The biblical story of Abraham and Isaac, found in Genesis 22, gets to me every time I read it. It's a story that is mysterious, thrilling, suspenseful, and joyous all at once. It's also a story that is convicting, because I put myself in the place of the father and ask, "What would I do?" This story clearly shows what I'm talking about: a parent trusting in the sovereign God for the life of his child.

The account begins with a test, and what a test it is! It's a test that I'm afraid I would fail epically.

> After these things God tested Abraham and said to him, "Abraham!" And he said, "Here I am." He said, "Take your son, your only son Isaac, whom you love, and go to the land of Moriah, and offer him there as a burnt offering on one of the mountains of which I shall tell you." So Abraham rose early in the morning, saddled his donkey, and took two of his young men with him, and his son Isaac. And he cut the wood for the burnt offering and arose and went to the place of which God had told him. . . . So they went both of them together. And Isaac said to his father Abraham, "My father!" And he said, "Here I am, my son." He said, "Behold, the fire and the wood, but where is the lamb for a burnt offering?" Abraham said, "God will provide for himself the lamb for a burnt offering, my son." So they went both of them together. (vv. 1–3, 6–8)

Every time I read this passage I feel like I'm reading a thriller novel, wondering what will happen in the end, even though I already know the outcome. When I'm finished reading, I have to sit and ponder God's ways because they are truly mysterious.

First, let's look at the characters. There are really only three in this story: Abraham, Isaac, and God. Abraham has already been called by God to do some fairly unusual things, and God has promised to make Abraham a great nation (Gen. 12:2–3; 15:5–6). Abraham proved to be a faithful follower of Yahweh, especially after he and his wife, Sarah, were blessed with a son, Isaac, long after their childbearing years were over.

Isaac is clearly a gift from God to his parents (Gen. 21:1–7). Although Abraham had another son, Ishmael, through his concubine Hagar, the Bible calls Isaac his "only son" (22:2). Because of Sarah's jealousy, Hagar and Ishmael are sent away, and God promises offspring to Abraham through Isaac (21:14). In Genesis 22, we see that Isaac and Abraham have a very special relationship—Isaac places complete trust in his father to carry out the plan they are about to enact.

God is the third person in this story, and as Yahweh, Creator God, he has ultimate authority in the lives of both Abraham and Isaac. God has proven himself faithful to Abraham in the past, he has established a covenantal relationship with Abraham, and he has provided Abraham with a son. In so doing he has gained the full trust of his servant. So when, at the beginning of Genesis 22, God calls Abraham, it comes as no surprise that Abraham immediately responds, "Here I am" (v. 1).

What *is* a surprise is what God asks Abraham to do next: "Take your son, your only son Isaac, whom you love, and go to the land of Moriah, and offer him there as a burnt offering on one of the mountains of which I shall tell you" (v. 2).

God doesn't say, "Offer a burnt offering" in general, or even, "Take a lamb for a burnt offering." He makes it abundantly clear that Abraham is to "offer him," Isaac, as the burnt offering. I can't imagine how Abraham's heart must have dropped at hearing these words, especially after knowing that God understood the depth of his love for his son, his only son. God is asking Abraham to prove his love, his loyalty, his allegiance, his complete trust in him—the One who has proven himself a faithful covenant-maker and promise-keeper for all the years that Abraham has followed him.

Another surprise: the scene is remarkably calm. Abraham and Isaac make preparations for the sacrifice and head out on a long journey to the place God has designated. We don't sense any struggle here—Abraham does not plead with God to do this another way, and Isaac does not struggle to avoid being placed on the altar. Even when Isaac questions his father, "Where is the lamb for a burnt offering?" (v. 7), Abraham replies, "God will provide for himself the lamb for a burnt offering, my son" (v. 8). I imagine Abraham looking straight ahead, eyes fixed on the path God had laid out for them, climbing the mountain toward the place where he would build the altar.

Perhaps you know the rest of the story. Abraham builds the altar, places Isaac upon it, and lifts a knife to kill his son. Just when things are looking bleakest, an angel of the Lord calls out, "Abraham, Abraham!" and, of course, Abraham quickly responds, "Here I am," because this is what Abraham has been conditioned, through years of obedience, to say. The angel of the Lord tells Abraham not to lay a hand on Isaac because "now I know that you fear God, seeing you have not withheld your son, your only son, from me" (v. 12).

Abraham has passed the test. He has trusted God with that which was most precious to him—his only son. Hebrews 11:19 tells us that Abraham believed God could raise Isaac from the dead. He had faith to see beyond this earthly life, and he understood that, even in tragedy or death, we have an ultimate and eternal hope. This calls to mind another "only son" in the Bible—Jesus. He was the ultimate sacrifice, and God the Father, because of his great love for us, gave his only Son so that we could live (John 3:16). God knows the love of a father's heart for his son, and because of this we can trust him.

What's Holding You Back?

If anything at all would get in the way of our believing that God has our best in mind, we must let it go. God knows how much we love our children, just as he knew Abraham's love for Isaac, but he also knows that this love and these children can easily become idols in our lives, and so we must begin, even when they are young, to loosen our grip on them. Sarah Young, in *Jesus Calling*, says this so well: "Entrust your loved ones to Me; release them into My protective care. They are much safer with Me than in your clinging hands. . . . I detest idolatry, even in the form of parental love."[6]

> ## We must begin, even when they are young, to loosen our grip on them.

As Young clearly points out, God hates idolatry. Don't believe her? Just read the Old Testament. Over and over again, God measures out unimaginable punishment on his chosen people because of their unfaithfulness to him. Earlier I mentioned the many sins of Hophni and Phinehas, the sons of Eli the priest mentioned in 1 Samuel 2. In that chapter, God confronts Eli for his less-than-favorable parenting skills, but what caused Eli the most trouble was his attitude toward his children. In 1 Samuel 2:29, the Lord says, "Why do you give your sons more honor than you give me?" (NLT). I don't know about you, but those words give me pause. When we put the needs, wants, or desires of our children above our commitment to God, we create idols out of them. And God sees it.

Author and pastor Jonathan Parnell further cautions parents against making their children into idols, saying, "Idols are always a cover-up for self-worship. When children become our idols, it means they become the means to our meaning."[7] And this is exactly what God detests. Self-worship, child-worship—any type of worship that is not directed solely toward a just and loving God is false worship.

September 11 changed parenting forever. Here's why. I believe that on that day, many parents, for the first time ever, began parenting out of fear. Some wrestled with their fear ("I'm not going to let the terrorists win") and won. Others wrestled their fears and gave in to them, deciding, whether consciously or subconsciously, to hold their children unreasonably close.

All in the name of safety.

This is a battle I have fought within myself so many times, but God has convicted me that I cannot—I must not—parent out of fear. So when my freshman in high school wants to take the train into Chicago with a group of friends, I ask who is going, make sure an older brother of one of the girls will be with them at all times, and I conquer my fear by saying yes. When, in college, this same adventurous daughter wants to drive to Alabama to the home of one of her friends for spring break, I talk it through with her, taking into account her abilities and her maturity (and those of her friends), and agree to let her take my car.

These decisions are never easy for a parent, but they are important steps, both for our kids and for us, in letting go. I'm not saying that bad things won't happen—I know from experience that they can and do. I'm also not saying we should be irresponsible regarding the safety of our children. What I am saying is what I learned when our friends planted a church in Chicago: our children are so much safer in God's protective care than in ours.

When we try to hold our kids back, not encouraging their gifts or, worse yet, discouraging them from trying new things, we start to play God in their lives. When we trust only in what we think is best, we and our children miss out on the abundant gifts that God is just waiting to shower on them.

Why Let Go?

First, I truly believe that the process of letting go is for our good as parents. When we release our grip, we are free to entrust our children into God's care and to grow our trust in him. This isn't easy, I know. When our oldest daughter, Kate, turned ten, my husband and I agreed to send her to summer camp for two weeks, but with my history, sending a child to camp was no easy thing. That day was one of the hardest days of my life, but it was an important one because it led me to greater trust in God's care for my daughter.

Through the years, our three girls have spent many summers at what has become one of our favorite places: HoneyRock Camp in Eagle River, Wisconsin. Each of my daughters has been encouraged in her faith there, and because of their experiences at HoneyRock, they have all developed leadership qualities that have served them well. Several years ago a blogger friend of mine, who is also a believer in Jesus, asked Julia this insightful question: "Aside from your parents, what has been the biggest influence on your faith?" Julia thought about her answer for a minute and then said, "I'd have to say my years at HoneyRock have taught me about God and have helped form my faith the most."

In that moment, I silently gave thanks to the Lord for enabling me to trust him enough to send my girls to summer camp. I knew the risks—that they could get hurt . . . or worse. Losing my brother taught me that I could not keep my children safe all the time. But I also knew that our loving heavenly Father was watching over them and that he could be trusted to care for my girls while they were away from me—no matter what happened. Without those camp experiences, Julia's faith would not be what it is today—she confirmed that.

What do I ultimately want as a parent? It's not my child's comfort or even her safety. What I ultimately want is what is best for her—a vibrant, growing, trusting faith in Jesus. While difficult and sometimes heartbreaking, letting my children go is what will ultimately be for their good and for mine.

Second, our letting go is for God's glory. I believe that when we intentionally loosen our grip on our children, when we make the story about him and not us, we bring glory to God.

Parenting is a story about God. As I said earlier in this book, our families are designed to reflect his grace, his redemptive story, to the world around us. Even this difficult step of letting go reflects God's character, because he performed the ultimate act of letting go by sending his Son, Jesus, into the world. When we hold our children with open hands, we can be sure that God is right beside us, encouraging us and helping us, because he knows how it feels.

Furthermore, when our children follow God's calling, first into salvation and then into their sanctification, they glorify God by sharing him with the world around them. If we don't let them go, if we hold them back, how can God's glory be proclaimed in the world?

As my daughters have heard me say throughout their lives, we are not here to take up space. We are here to use the gifts God has given us to benefit those around us and, ultimately, to bring glory to him. Holding our children back by not letting go, not opening our hands to what God has for our kids, may hold back gifts that the world needs.

Think of the gifts your children possess. Think of the hurting world that needs those gifts. And choose, today, to bless the world by letting go.

God's Provision

The story of Abraham doesn't end with the angel of the Lord holding back Abraham's hand from Isaac's throat. There's more to it than that: "And Abraham lifted up his eyes and looked, and behold, behind him was a ram, caught in a thicket by his horns. And Abraham went and took the ram and offered it up as a burnt offering instead of his son. So Abraham called the name of that place, 'The LORD will provide'; as it is said to this day, 'On the mount of the LORD it shall be provided'" (Gen. 22:13–14).

God provides a new sacrifice, a substitute for Isaac that is both miraculous and mysterious. Abraham looks over and finds a ram stuck by his horns in some bushes nearby, so he offers the ram as the burnt offering instead of his son.

What grace! What provision! There is no denying that the fingerprints of God are all over this story. This story foreshadows God sacrificing his only Son, "the Lamb of God" (John 1:29), for the sins of the world. We are *supposed* to see Jesus. Those of us who live in the age of the New Testament are supposed to read this story and be amazed that all those years earlier, all those generations back, God had already planned a perfect sacrifice to meet the need of the world.

> **God, who loves our children dearly, has made provision for them through his Son.**

Friends, we don't know the trials our children may face along the journey. But what we do know is that God, who loves our children dearly, has made provision for them through his Son. We know that he will care for our children just as he cared for Isaac. Matthew Henry says this about Genesis 22: "God, by his word, calls us to part with all for Christ . . . all those things that are competitors and rivals with Christ for the sovereignty of the heart (Luke 14:26); and we must cheerfully let them all go."[8] Can we, as those who claim faith in God, honestly say we cannot let go?

Parents, I know that some of you are struggling with this. I know because I've struggled with it, and I talk to parents every day who struggle with it too. We must ask ourselves, "Do I really believe in the sovereignty of God in the lives of my children?" and, "Am I willing to cheerfully part with all for Christ?" These are probably two of the most difficult questions any parent could ask, but as the story of Abraham and Isaac proves, God is faithful—always. And we can trust him to write the story of our children in the most beautiful, life-affirming, God-honoring way.

He is good. He is sovereign. He can be trusted.

Consider

1. Why do you think letting go is important? Is it important to include this in your family's travel plan? Why or why not?
2. What makes it hard for you to intentionally let go of your children?
3. In what areas of your child's life could you be trusting God more? In what areas do you need to let go of control?
4. Read the following verses: Deuteronomy 6:4–5; Joshua 1:9; Psalm 118:6; Proverbs 18:10; John 3:16. Choose one to claim this week as you process letting go. Write it in the space below.

CONCLUSION

My greatest fear in writing a book about parenting has been that some may come away from it discouraged, thinking they've just been given a to-do list for parenting. Some may read this book and think, *That's so much to do! So much to remember! What if I fail?*

I talk to parents every week who have questions, fears, and regrets. They have made mistakes (who hasn't?), and they wonder if they're cut out for the job. These are some of the things I've worried about myself. I've been worn-out, weary, frustrated, and upset with my lack of patience and ability.

And yet, God repeatedly reminds me that I am my daughters' mother. There is no one else who could do that job. And because God has given me this job to do, I can trust that he will also equip me to do it.

I know that in your heart you want to do the job right, whatever *right* means. You want children who know and love Jesus, and quite possibly you want some magic formula to make sure that happens. There is no magic formula, much as I wish there were. But does that mean we just give up trying to intentionally instill the values we know are foundational to our child's faith? No. We keep going, and we recognize that God will help us fulfill our obligations.

o O o

A passage in the book of Job seems to sum up parenthood well. Job has hit on some hard times—he's lost everything, literally everything—so he sits with his friends, grieving, and he asks some pretty demanding questions of God. After all of Job's questioning and his friends' incompetent answering, God finally speaks up. He, in return, puts some pretty tough questions to Job, beginning with this one: "Where were you when I laid the foundation of the earth? Tell me, if you have understanding" (Job 38:4). And the questions that prove God's authority and power continue.

In chapter 39 God challenges Job with words that strike this mama's heart:

> Do you know when the mountain goats give birth?
>   Do you observe the calving of the does?
> Can you number the months that they fulfill,
>   and do you know the time when they give birth,
> when they crouch, bring forth their offspring,
>   and are delivered of their young?
> Their young ones become strong; they grow up in the open;
>   they go out and do not return to them.
>
> (vv. 1–4)

Here is life in God's nutshell: birth, growth, and leaving. It's wonderful, fulfilling, and heartbreaking all at once. As a mom and brand-new empty nester, these words cut deep, as the leaving part makes me feel a bit tender right now.

Here is life in God's nutshell: birth, growth, and leaving. It's wonderful, fulfilling, and heartbreaking.

But the great thing I take away is that God sees it all. He knows when the mountain goat gives birth. He sees when a doe has her offspring. He knows the number of their days, watches as they grow, and observes when they leave their mother.

Birth. Growth. Leaving. And all the days in between.

If God notices the life of the deer and the mountain goat, doesn't he surely notice you?

He sees your struggling child and loves him.

He sees your daughter with disabilities and loves her.

He sees the child who finds it a challenge to make friends or who has a hard time in school, and he loves him.

He sees you, Mom and Dad, with your bleary-eyed exhaustion after another challenging day juggling work and kids, and he loves you too.

And, while we can only see the small moments in front of us, moments that we fear will ruin our child forever, God sees the whole picture from beginning to end. I find great comfort in knowing that God sees and knows everything about my children and my family and loves us still.

o O o

So where do we go from here? You may feel overwhelmed after reading this, as if the job of discipling your kids is much too big for you. You know what? You're right. It is too big. And that's why God gave us his Holy Spirit to help us, guide us, and teach us. I suggest that you begin to pray diligently about the areas of growth and discipleship that he wants to see in your child. It may be something I've mentioned here, but it could be something that's not even in this book. God may have a special lesson that only your child needs to learn. Pray about what God wants for your child and for your family.

Let me also say that Rome (or the Wildman family) wasn't built in a day. My children are now in their twenties, so we've been at this for a while. Some lessons took me years to learn, and I'm still learning others. The teaching, the praying, and the discipling never really end. The work takes on different forms, but it never stops—I'm on my knees for my children more these days than I've ever been. I hope that I will always have the privilege of speaking into the lives of my daughters.

Because spiritual development takes time, and because it can be overwhelming, I'd suggest choosing two or three areas that I've discussed here to pray through for your kids. And keep asking why! Why is this value important for this child at this time? Why are we doing what we're doing as a family? Why are we not doing what we don't do?

Finally, consider writing out your family's unique purpose with your values in mind. It can be as simple as writing out three or four statements—"We are _____"—and posting them on your refrigerator for everyone to see. Take some time to develop these ideas together and see how God begins to focus and transform your family.

And remember: God wants to work through you to connect your child with his Son. That's it. Everything else we do is secondary to this connection with Christ. What I've tried to do here is simply give you some ideas of ways you can foster that connection. If you can implement one or two ideas from this book or think of another idea for purposefully investing yourself in discipling your child, that's enough. Don't get overwhelmed by trying to do too much. Just focus on the first priority: that connection with Jesus.

As Paul Tripp puts it,

> Parenting is *ambassadorial* work from beginning to end. It is not to be shaped and directed by personal interest, personal need, or cultural perspectives. Every parent everywhere is called to recognize that they have been put on earth at a particular time and in a particular location to do one thing in the lives of their children. What is that one thing? It is God's will. Here's what this means at street level: parenting is not first about what we want *for* our children or *from* our children, but about what God in grace has planned to do through us *in* our children.[1]

In other words, our job as parents is to do the will of God by bringing our children to him and him to our children, every day, at every opportunity.

Intentionally.

In the end, we will stand before our Judge and he will ask what we did with the gifts and opportunities and days we'd been given. Did we steward well the children he gave us? And by that I don't mean, did our kids get into the right schools, achieve a high level at their sport, or get academic awards. I mean, did we remember every day to focus on the first priority?

Did we help our children know, beyond a shadow of a doubt, that they are loved, deeply loved, by their heavenly Father? Did we help our children recognize their sin, and along with that, did we show them the grace that we've been shown? Did we help our children understand that they too are stewards of their lives and responsible to leave an indelible mark on those around them? Did we teach them to be kind, generous, and helpful to others?

These values are matters of the heart, and these types of values are what really matter. Birthday parties and organic food and the "right schools" don't matter one bit in the end. But who our children are becoming and who we ourselves are becoming do matter. Let's be the people God wants us to be, and let's intentionally invest in our own spiritual lives and in the spiritual lives of our children, so that God can one day look us in the eye and say, "Well done."

APPENDIX

Some Helpful Financial Resources

CNN Money, http://money.cnn.com/pf/money-essentials/—For parents who need a primer on money management.

Consumer Financial Protection Bureau, http://www.consumerfinance.gov/money-as-you-grow/—Age-appropriate sections with activities and conversation starters.

The Mint, http://www.themint.org—A practical tool for learning money management with sections for kids, teens, parents, and teachers.

Ramsey Solutions, http://www.daveramsey.com/blog/9-ways-to-teach-your-kids-about-money—Dave Ramsey has several good resources for teaching kids (and adults) about money.

Three Jars, http://www.threejars.com—An interactive tool where parents can make deposits into a child's account, and the child can learn to give, save, and spend.

NOTES

Chapter 1: Discipleship 101

1. Paul Tripp, *Parenting: 14 Gospel Principles That Can Radically Change Your Family* (Wheaton, IL: Crossway, 2016), 54.

Chapter 2: Families Are Like Road Trips

1. John DeFrain and Sylvia M. Asay, "Strong Families Around the World: An Introduction to the Family Strengths Perspective" in *Strong Families Around the World: Strengths-Based Research and Perspectives*, ed. John DeFrain and Sylvai M. Asay (Philadelphia: Haworth Press, 2007), 2.
2. Froma Walsh, "Family Resilience: A Framework for Clinical Practice," *Family Process* 42, no. 1 (Spring 2003): 1.
3. Theresa J. Early and Linnea F. GlenMaye, "Valuing Families: Social Work Practice with Families from a Strengths Perspective," *Social Work* 45, no. 2 (March 2000): n.p., http://www.biomedsearch.com/article /Valuing-Families-Social-Work-Practice/60470924.html.
4. Richard A. Easterlin, "The Economics of Happiness," *Daedalus* 133, no. 2 (Spring 2004): 26.
5. Joan Chittister, *Happiness* (Grand Rapids: Eerdmans, 2011), 19.
6. Paul Tripp, *Parenting: 14 Gospel Principles That Can Radically Change Your Family* (Wheaton, IL: Crossway, 2016), 30.
7. Margaret Feinberg, *Scouting the Divine: My Search for God in Wine, Wool, and Wild Honey* (Grand Rapids: Zondervan, 2009), 55.
8. Easterlin, "Economics of Happiness," 32.
9. Chick-fil-A, "Corporate Purpose," accessed January 11, 2018, https:// www.chick-fil-a.com/About/Who-We-Are.
10. Bruce Feiler, *The Secrets of Happy Families: Improve Your Mornings, Re-think Family Dinner, Fight Smarter, Go Out and Play, and Much More* (New York: William Morrow, 2013), 191–92.

Chapter 3: The Problem with Triangles

1. Terrie E. Moffitt, Richie Poulton, and Avshalom Caspi, "Lifelong Impact of Early Self-Control," *American Scientist* 101, no. 6 (September/October 2013): 355.
2. Charles Duhigg, *The Power of Habit: Why We Do What We Do in Life and Business* (New York: Random House, 2014), 133.
3. Moffitt, Poulton, and Caspi, "Lifelong Impact," 355.
4. Jonah Lehrer, "Don't! The Secret of Self-Control," *The New Yorker*, May 18, 2009, http://pen.memberlodge.org/resources/Documents/Secret(s)%20of%20Self-Control.pdf.
5. Moffitt, Poulton, and Caspi, "Lifelong Impact," 355.
6. Duhigg, *Power of Habit*, 137.
7. Duhigg, 139.

Chapter 4: He Is Here, and He Hears

1. Bill Hybels, *Too Busy Not to Pray* (Downers Grove, IL: InterVarsity Press, 1998), 12.
2. Dietrich Bonhoeffer, *The Cost of Discipleship* (New York: Macmillan, 1963), 183.
3. "God's Faithfulness: Bread & Milk," Müllers, accessed January 11, 2018, mullers.org/find-out-more-1837.
4. Tony Reinke, "10 Questions on Prayer with Tim Keller," *Desiring God*, October 31, 2014, http://www.desiringgod.org/articles/10-questions-on-prayer-with-tim-keller.
5. Christina Fox, "The Most Frightening Prayer I Could Pray for My Children," *Desiring God*, July 17, 2013, http://www.desiringgod.org/articles/the-most-frightening-prayer-i-could-pray-for-my-children.

Chapter 5: Loving Our Team

1. C. S. Lewis, *Letters to Malcolm: Chiefly on Prayer* (New York: Harcourt, 1964), 10.
2. Richard Foster, *Celebration of Discipline: The Path to Spiritual Growth* (New York: Harper & Row, 1978), 158.
3. Josh Moody, *How Church Can Change Your Life: Answers to the Ten Most*

Common Questions About Church (Fearn, Scotland: Christian Focus, 2015), v–vi.

4. Donald Miller, "I Don't Worship God by Singing. I Connect with Him Elsewhere," *Storyline*, accessed January 11, 2018, http://storylineblog .com/2014/02/03/i-dont-worship-god-by-singing-i-connect-with-him -elsewhere/.

5. Foster, *Celebration of Discipline*, 172–73.

6. Kent and Barbara Hughes, *Common Sense Parenting* (Wheaton, IL: Tyndale, 1995), 73.

7. James K. A. Smith, *You Are What You Love: The Spiritual Power of Habit* (Grand Rapids: Brazos, 2016), 57.

8. Smith, 128.

9. John Piper, "The Family: Together in God's Presence," *Desiring God*, January 1, 1995, https://www.desiringgod.org/articles/the-family-together -in-gods-presence.

10. "What Millennials Want When They Visit Church," Barna Group, March 4, 2015, https://barna.org/barna-update/millennials/711-what -millennials-want-when-they-visit-church#.V5D4CCNRQ01.

11. "5 Reasons Millennials Stay Connected to Church," Barna Group, September 17, 2013, https://barna.org/barna-update/millennials/635-5 -reasons-millennials-stay-connected-to-church#.VuwnR2TR_C4.

12. "U.S. Public Becoming Less Religious," Pew Research Center, November 3, 2015, http://www.pewforum.org/2015/11/03/u-s-public-becom ing-less-religious/.

13. "Religion Among the Millennials," Pew Research Center, February 17, 2010, http://www.pewforum.org/2010/02/17/religion-among-the -millennials/.

14. Jon Nielson, *Faith That Lasts: Raising Kids That Don't Leave the Church* (Fort Washington, PA: CLC Publishers, 2016), 205.

15. Nielson, 209.

Chapter 6: "My Word Is My Bond"

1. "Corporate Responsibility," London Stock Exchange Group, accessed January 22, 2018, http://www.lseg.com/about-london-stock-exchange -group/corporate-responsibility.

2. Jessica Lahey, "Why Students Lie, and Why We Fall for It," *New York Times*, February 10, 2016, http://parenting.blogs.nytimes.com/2016/02/10/why-students-lie-and-why-we-fall-for-it/?_r=1.

3. Kang Lee, "Little Liars: Development of Verbal Deception in Children," *Child Development Perspectives* 7, no. 2 (2013): 91–96, https://www.ncbi.nlm.nih.gov/pmc/articles/PMC3653594/.

4. Angela D. Evans and Kang Lee, "Promising to Tell the Truth Makes 8- to 16-Year-Olds More Honest," *Behavioral Sciences & The Law* 28, no. 6 (2010): 801–11, https://www.ncbi.nlm.nih.gov/pmc/articles/PMC2992584/.

5. John Piper, "Is Lying Ever Okay for Christians?" *Relevant*, May 4, 2010, http://www.relevantmagazine.com/god/deeper-walk/features/21429-is-lying-ever-okay.

Chapter 7: Having Eyes to See

1. Melissa Chan, "Boy with Autism Who Ate Lunch with Football Player No Longer Sits Alone," *Time*, September 2, 2016, http://time.com/4478169/boy-autism-football-player-fsu-travis-rudolph-lunch-alone/.

2. "Fifth Graders Pledge to Protect 'Special Needs' Boy on the Playground," Good News Network, June 2, 2015, http://www.goodnewsnetwork.org/fifth-graders-pledge-to-protect-special-needs-boy-on-the-playground-must-see/.

3. James Matthew Wilson, "Remembering Brett Foster," *First Things*, November 19, 2015, https://www.firstthings.com/blogs/firstthoughts/2015/11/remembering-brett-foster.

4. C. S. Lewis, *Mere Christianity* (New York: Simon & Schuster, 1996), 116.

5. R. J. Palacio, *Wonder* (New York: Random House, 2012), 48.

Chapter 8: Heart Work

1. Daniela Acquadro Maran et al., "Serving Others and Gaining Experience: A Study of University Students Participation in Service Learning," *Higher Education Quarterly* 63, no. 1 (January 2009): 52, doi: 10.1111/j.1468-2273.2008.00407.x.

2. Richard Foster, *Celebration of Discipline: The Path to Spiritual Growth*, 3rd ed. (San Francisco: HarperSanFrancisco, 1998), 126–27.

Chapter 9: Money Matters

1. Lisa Smith, "The No. 1 Reason Why Couples Fight," *Investopedia*, accessed January 11, 2018, http://www.investopedia.com/articles/pf/07/couples-finance.asp.

2. Jill M. Norvilitis and Michael G. MacLean, "The Role of Parents in College Students' Financial Behaviors and Attitudes," *Journal of Economic Psychology* 31 (February 2010): 55–63, doi: 10.1016/j.joep.2009.10.003.

3. Adam M. Hancock, Bryce L. Jorgensen, and Melvin S. Swanson, "College Students and Credit Card Use: The Role of Parents, Work Experience, Financial Knowledge, and Credit Card Attitudes," *Journal of Economic and Family Issues* 34, no. 4 (December 2013): 369–81, doi: 10.1007/s10834-012-9338-8.

4. Angela C. Lyons, "A Profile of Financially At-Risk College Students," *Journal of Consumer Affairs* 38, no. 1 (2004): 56–80, doi: 10.1111/j.1745-6606.2004.tb00465.x.

5. Sonya Britt, "The Intergenerational Transference of Money Attitudes and Behaviors," *Journal of Consumer Affairs* 50, no. 3 (2016): 539–56, doi: 10.1111/joca.12113.

6. Britt, 544.

7. Matthew Henry, "Matthew 6," *Matthew Henry's Commentary on the Whole Bible*, Bible Study Tools, accessed January 11, 2018, http://www.biblestudytools.com/commentaries/matthew-henry-complete/matthew/6.html.

8. Quentin Fottrell, "Most Americans Are One Paycheck Away from the Street," *Marketwatch*, January 31, 2016, http://www.marketwatch.com/story/most-americans-are-one-paycheck-away-from-the-street-2016-01-06.

Chapter 10: Strengthening Our Ties

1. David King and Margot Starbuck, *Overplayed: A Parent's Guide to Sanity in the World of Youth Sports* (Harrisonburg, VA: Herald Press, 2016), 24.

2. King and Starbuck, 24–25.

3. King and Starbuck, 28.

4. Robert Lowry, "Nothing but the Blood," 1876, public domain.

5. Bruce Feiler, *The Secrets of Happy Families: Improve Your Mornings, Rethink Family Dinner, Fight Smarter, Go Out and Play, and Much More* (New York: William Morrow, 2013), 35.

6. Feiler, 41–42.

Chapter 11: Same but Different

1. Harriet Sherwood, "People of No Religion Outnumber Christians in England and Wales—Study," *Guardian*, May 23, 2016, https://www.theguardian.com/world/2016/may/23/no-religion-outnumber-christians-england-wales-study.

2. Mariela Dabbah, "What is Cultural Sensitivity?" *Red Shoe Movement*, accessed January 11, 2018, http://redshoemovement.com/what-is-cultural-sensitivity/.

3. Harper Lee, *To Kill a Mockingbird* (New York: Harper Perennial Modern Classics, 2002), 33.

Chapter 12: The Long Walk Toward Trust

1. Gaia Berenstein and Zvi Triger, "Over-Parenting," *UC Davis Law Review* 44 (2011): 1227.

2. Berenstein and Triger, 1225.

3. Judith Locke, Marilyn A. Campbell, and David J. Kavanagh, "Can a Parent Do Too Much for Their Child? An Examination by Parenting Professionals of the Concept of Overparenting," *Australian Journal of Guidance and Counselling* 22, no. 2 (2012): 4.

4. Judith Warner, *Perfect Madness: Motherhood in the Age of Anxiety* (New York: Penguin, 2005), 29.

5. Hara Estroff Marano, "A Nation of Wimps," Psychology Today, November 1, 2004, https://www.psychologytoday.com/articles/200411/nation-wimps.

6. Sarah Young, *Jesus Calling* (Nashville: Thomas Nelson, 2004), 246.

7. Jonathan Parnell, "Parenting Means Wrestling Demons," *Desiring God*, March 4, 2015, http://www.desiringgod.org/articles/parenting-means-wrestling-demons.

8. Matthew Henry, "Genesis 22," *Matthew Henry's Commentary on the*

Whole Bible, Bible Study Tools, accessed January 11, 2018, http://www
.biblestudytools.com/commentaries/matthew-henry-complete/genesis
/22.html.

Conclusion

1. Paul Tripp, *Parenting: 14 Gospel Principles That Can Radically Change
Your Family* (Wheaton, IL: Crossway, 2016), 14–15.

ABOUT THE AUTHOR

SHELLY WILDMAN IS AN AUTHOR, SPEAKER, AND FORMER WRITING professor who is passionate about raising the next generation for Christ. She speaks frequently to women's groups and spends much of her free time mentoring young women. Shelly holds degrees from Wheaton College (BA) and the University of Illinois at Chicago (MA), but her most important life's work has been raising her three daughters. She and her husband, Brian, have been married for thirty-two years and live in Wheaton, Illinois. Connect with Shelly online at www.shellywildman. com.